PENGUIN BOOKS

THE KIND FOOD GUIDE

Audrey Eyton is the author of *The F-Plan Diet* which holds the record for being the fastest selling book of all time in Britain. It sold more copies than any other non-fiction book in Britain in the 1980s and went on to become a worldwide bestseller. It is credited with having made lasting changes to our national eating habits.

She can also claim the credit for having invented that now popular feature of every magazine stall, the slimming magazine. When she co-founded and edited *Slimming Magazine*, more than twenty years ago, it was the first publication in the world to specialize in the subject.

Her twenty years of experience in writing about nutrition in relation to weight problems made her well aware of the massive error of post-war nutritional policy, which encouraged the dangerous over-consumption of meat and dairy products. From there it was a short step to discover the wider implications of our 'cheap meat' policy for animals and the environment, as well as for human health.

In recent years she has lived for most of the time in her cottage in the country, where she researches, writes and 'gardens with passion' in her spare time. She has a student son, a dog and two cats.

D1150062

THE KIND FOOD GUIDE

AUDREY EYTON

PENGUIN BOOKS

PENGUIN BOOKS

Published by the Penguin Group
Penguin Books Ltd, 27 Wrights Lane, London w8 5tz, England
Viking Penguin, a division of Penguin Books USA Inc.
375 Hudson Street, New York, New York 10014, USA
Penguin Books Australia Ltd, Ringwood, Victoria, Australia
Penguin Books Canada Ltd, 2801 John Street, Markham, Ontario, Canada l3r 1b4
Penguin Books (NZ) Ltd, 182–190 Wairau Road, Auckland 10, New Zealand

Penguin Books Ltd, Registered Offices: Harmondsworth, Middlesex, England

First published 1991

Copyright © Audrey Eyton, 1991
All rights reserved

The moral right of the author has been asserted

Printed in England by Clays Ltd, St Ives plc
Set in 10/12 Monophoto Baskerville

Except in the United States of America,
this book is sold subject to the condition
that it shall not, by way of trade or otherwise,
be lent, re-sold, hired out, or otherwise circulated
without the publisher's prior consent in any form of
binding or cover other than that in which it is
published and without a similar condition
including this condition being imposed
on the subsequent purchaser

Dedicated to the memory of my mother, Evelyn Gray, who had a most tender concern for all living creatures, and was my warm supporter in the early stages of my work on this book

CONTENTS

Acknowledgements ix

PART ONE: INTRODUCTION   1
  1. Watch Out for German U-boats!   9
  2. Exclusive Interviews with Pigs, Hens and
       Sheep 15
  3. A Message from God to John Gummer . . . 23
     The Stay-alive Guide 33
  4. Four Hundred Million Further Reasons
       for Eating Less Meat 43
  5. Please Don't Try Too Hard 47

**PART TWO: GUIDE TO THE KINDER
ALTERNATIVES** 53
  6. The Cruellest Foods of All 61
  7. Also Factory-farmed 87
  8. Highly Questionable 91
  9. Questionable 103
     The Healthiest Diet Known to Science (colour
       section between pages 116 and 117)
 10. Foods You Can Feel Better About 117
     *Down Your Aisle – An At-a-glance Guide to
       the Supermarkets* 129
     Home Delivery Services 139

**PART THREE: THE A TO Z OF
EDIBLE ANIMALS** 143

ACKNOWLEDGEMENTS

I T would be difficult to name all the helpful people who have provided information for this book – and for some, my public thanks might not prove to be an altogether unmixed blessing. For these reasons I have refrained from naming the experts from the Ministry of Agriculture, Fisheries and Food who supplied me with so many fascinating facts.

All of the following have been particularly helpful, either in specific areas of my research or in providing overall guidance, and I am deeply grateful to them:

Veterinary experts: Alastair Mews, Head of the RSPCA's Farm Animal Department, has burned much midnight oil providing and checking my facts. My thanks also to his colleague, Martin Potter, and his predecessor, John Douglas; also to G. B. S. Heath and our own splendid family vet, David Redfern, who has taught me a great deal.

Academics and scientists: Professor John Webster, of Bristol University's School of Veterinary Science, has been enormously generous with his own time in helping me with information for the A–Z guide. I am particularly indebted to him. Donald Broom, Colleen Macleod

ACKNOWLEDGEMENTS

Professor of Animal Welfare at Cambridge University, opened my eyes to the true nature of farm animals. I thoroughly recommend his book *Farm Animal Behaviour and Welfare*, published by Baillière Tindall, to those who wish to learn more about this subject. My thanks also to the aptly named Dr David Jones and his colleagues at Bangor University's School of Ocean Science, Professor David Wood-Gush of Edinburgh University, Dr Neville Gregory, Dr Christine Nichol, Dr Mike Baxter and Dr Alan Long.

Nutritional and medical experts: I am very grateful to Professor Sir Richard Doll, of Oxford, for his guidance on dietary causes of cancer, and to my old friends Professor Philip James, Director of the Rowett Research Institute (and Chairman of the Coronary Prevention Group), Dr Catherine Geissler, who heads London University's Department of Nutrition, Dr David Southgate, of the AFRC Institute of Food Research, and Professor Theodore Van Itallie, of New York.

Welfarists: Joyce D'Silva and her colleagues at Compassion in World Farming have been a tireless source of information and inspiration. I am also grateful to the remarkable Clare Druce (a living dictionary of information on poultry), Roger Ewbank, of the Universities Federation for Animal Welfare, Ruth Harrison of the Farm Animal Welfare Council, John Bryant of the League Against Cruel Sports, Sir Cameron Rusby of the Scottish Society for the Prevention of Cruelty to Animals and Lara Calthorpe of the World Society for the Protection of Animals.

Environmentalists: Charles Nodder of the Game Conservancy gave much help in providing and checking facts, and I am also grateful to Dr John Harrodine of the British Association of Shooting and Conservation, Catherine Barr of Greenpeace, Nick Davis of the Whale and Dolphin Conservation Society and Frances Blake and colleagues of the Soil Association.

Others: Among many other people who have helped are Sir Richard Body, Sir Julian Rose, Katie Thear of *Home Farm Magazine*, Alison Johnson, Richard Farhall, Ian Mather and John Gale of Folkestone Trawlers, who patiently answered so many questions on so many occasions.

Factory farmers: I think it better not to name them, but I am grateful to those who had the honesty to show me their systems of animal rearing and talk frankly about welfare aspects clearly worrying them as well as me. In such producers, rather than those who lock their factory doors and deny the horrors inside, lies the best hope of swift change for the better.

Friends and neighbours: Finally, my warmest thanks to my friends and neighbours Grace, Phyllis, Sylvia and Margaret who were always willing to look after my own animals so that I could go off to see the unloved farm animals.

PART ONE

INTRODUCTION

INTRODUCTION

There is More than One Way Not to Skin a Rabbit!

I N 1987 my son announced that he was no longer going to eat meat or poultry. This came as no surprise. My niece in Sheffield, a young relative in Wales, the boy who lives across the road in our village in Kent and so many of my friends' children had already made the same decision.

'It's such a bore, you have to make two sets of meals,' complained a woman at a dinner party about a similar situation in her own family. Priding myself on being as non-violent as the next woman, I was a little surprised by a sudden strong impulse to empty my soup in her lap.

Truth to tell, I felt some respect for these young people. For many years, whenever I thought of it, I had felt deeply discomforted by what was clearly going on in factory farming. So much so that I tried not to think about it at all. 'Oh, don't tell me, I can't bear to hear about it,' more or less summed up my own position. Pages in publications revealing factory-farming horrors were turned over swiftly. Ditto any television channel when a programme even touched on the subject. I was much too caring and sensitive a person to be able to cope with anything so distressing.

For a few months I continued to eat meat and poultry, when my son was away from home. But with decreasing relish. The hypocrisy and lack of logic of my position steadily dawned. Here was a new generation not afraid to look with clear eyes at the appalling cruelty to animals which has simply become an accepted part of our post-war life. And, much more important, so many of them were determined to do something about it, each in his own small way, by at least refusing to support the system.

I re-interpreted my own attitude. 'Oh, don't tell me, I can't bear to hear about it,' translates precisely to: 'Do what you want to animals, as long as you don't tell me.'

I decided to do something about it, myself.

For nearly three years I inveigled my way, by one means or another, into factory farms and talked with many hundreds of experts – vets, fishermen, nutritionists, agricultural scientists, environmentalists, welfarists, men from the ministry and, of course, the factory farmers themselves. What emerged was even worse than I had anticipated.

There was also, however, a most heartening discovery. Now, for the first time in all the post-war decades, there is a realistic possibility of ending the cruel practices of factory farming in Britain. Whether we end them or not depends not on politicians or agribusinessmen, thank goodness, but, quite simply, on us. And what we have to do, to put an end to this appalling era, is so little that it may surprise you.

Certainly, it is not necessary to turn vegetarian. (There is more than one way not to skin a rabbit!) Nor need you sacrifice sausages, bacon, poultry, beef or whatever animal edible turns you on, or stop shopping at those so-convenient chain stores and supermarkets. In fact, the supermarket-shopping omnivore can probably do more than anyone else, at the present time, to bring in a new era of healthier and more humane farming.

You may also be relieved to learn, as you embark on this book, that you don't necessarily have to read about those distressing details of factory-farming practices in order to bring about the changes. I have taken every care to protect your sensibilities.

A few overall truths are well worth facing, however. One is that today, in the second half of the 'civilized' twentieth century, we inflict more cruelty on animals than ever before in the history of man. The cock-fighters and bull-baiters of old could in no way compete with us in the barbaric treatment of helpless creatures. No doubt animals have been slaughtered brutally since meat-eating began. But never, until our own post-war age, have untold millions of them been confined for months, even years, in prolonged pain and suffering. For animals, these are the Dark Ages.

And to what purpose?

So that we, in the West, could embark on a unique and perilous experiment with our health. With the advent of cheap, intensively farmed animal products, our society has made an alarmingly sudden switch to a diet completely unnatural to man. The results are already manifest. Diet-related coronaries and cancers have now replaced the old infective illnesses and two thirds of us will die from these causes – many prematurely.

While we kill ourselves off with an excess of intensively farmed animal products, many people in the Third World are starving. 'The cattle of the rich steal the bread of the poor,' said Mahatma Gandhi. This is even more true today. Vast quantities of Third World crops are imported to feed our factory-farmed animals. By our extravagant habit of recycling so much cereal and other edible food through animals we waste about 90 per cent of the calories originally available. In doing so we drain them from a hungry world.

At the same time our eating practices pollute and endanger the planet. Tropical rainforests are chopped down mainly to provide land to rear more beef cattle for beefburgers. Factory farming is one of the major causes of pollution in the West: Denmark and the Netherlands, along with Britain, the most intensively farmed of the European countries, are rapidly submerging in a sea of slurry. Elections are even being fought on the issue.

Meanwhile, the soil in our fields, once replenished by grazing animals, is being eroded. Hedgerows, grown for centuries to contain these animals, are chopped down as being of no further use. With them goes the wildlife, robbed of its habitat and poisoned by the chemicals which are essential for intensive crop production – which in turn has become necessary in order to feed the millions of animals, imprisoned in dark sheds, which supply us with the cheap animal products that sustain our staggering rate of cancers and coronary heart attacks. Does this system make any sense to you?

Whatever may be said in public, the disaster of our post-war intensive agricultural policy is now openly acknowledged in the seats of learning and in the corridors of power. Only huge vested interests and cynical political concerns continue to sustain it.

Happily, two major forces for change are now at work. One is the new and nicer generation. The other is that other emerging species, 'the caring consumer'. If real change comes about, as it can, it will be consumer-led. The only weapon that counts is the shopping-bag. The whole purpose of this book is to show you how to wield yours.

You need do only two things in order to bring about a mighty change for the better. Eat less animal food and select what you do eat from the 'kinder' lines, now so easily available in the supermarkets. In doing so you will protect the health of yourself and your family, help to decrease Third World hunger, spare the rainforests, decrease pollution of rivers and seas, combat the world's great problem of desertification and soil erosion, protect what is left of our hedgerows, wildlife and countryside – and spare untold millions of helpless animals from prolonged suffering.

Were you ever offered more, for less?

1. WATCH OUT FOR GERMAN U-BOATS!

'**B**ELIEVE me,' says the factory farmer, with that look of sincerity directed straight into your eyes – or the lens of the television camera – 'you just can't produce meat (or eggs or milk) unless you treat your animals properly. It can't be done.'

We are tempted to believe him. After all, we are only too aware of being ignorant townies or country new-comers, and no one wants to sound like Linda Snell. Truth to tell, we rather want to believe him.

'Farmers don't go around being needlessly cruel to their animals,' he expounds, waxing indignant at the latest media exposé of factory farming. 'What would be the point?'

And, indeed, there he has a point. Farmers are not cruel for fun. Largely the cruelties lie in the system, rather than in the individual's treatment of individual animals. There even appeared to be some sensible pur-pose in factory farming when it all began, shortly after the Second World War.

Before the war, Britain had been producing only 30 per cent of its own food. During the war, with German U-boats threatening the ships bringing food to Britain, there was a very real danger of our being starved into submission – as those of us who 'dug for victory' and savoured 'Woolton pie' well recall.

On top of that, pre-war surveys revealed nutritional deficiencies among the poor. Some nutritionists (erroneously as it turned out) suspected that this was mainly due to insufficient protein. They concluded that what we needed in order to build up a stronger post-war generation was more food of animal origin. That was the stuff to give the children of the troops.

So, whether to fend off rickets or to protect ourselves from any future threat to our food supply, everyone was agreed that what we needed was more meat, eggs and dairy products, produced at less cost.

The post-war government swung into action with commendable vigour and unprecedented funds were allocated to agricultural research. The outcome was that the mixed farm, where animals grazed in the fields, was replaced by the huge factories we see today.

Certainly, this appeared to cut costs, in particular labour costs. Thousands of farm workers lost their jobs. Factories grew and grew into today's massive, highly automated units, where one man can 'look after' a hundred thousand chickens. At the same time, the animals were crowded closer and closer together. This, too, appeared to have economic advantages. Deprived of movement, the animals no longer burned up calories in unproductive expenditure of energy. Crowded so close, like people at a party, they generated enough heat to keep their bodies and the building warm. This saved further food, since calories are also normally used to keep up body temperature. Clever stuff! Indeed, the whole energy input–output equation was worked out with remarkable precision.

What somehow got left out of the calculations was that animals are living creatures, not machines –

creatures with their own behavioural needs and with the capacity to suffer. What post-war agricultural practice showed us was just how much we can get away with in mistreating them while (seemingly, at least) still obtaining the products we require from them.

As we are now beginning to discover, it is doubtful whether we can in fact get healthy meat from ill-treated animals. Certainly we can't get the tasty meat we used to enjoy. But we can and do get the soft, whitish, flavourless stuff which passes as pork and poultry today. Or the equally tasteless and increasingly suspect beef from intensive units.

Even humans can survive for some time when subject to the most severe suffering and deprivation, and 'farm' animals these days are required to live for only a very short time. Today's fast-food philosophy begins on the farm with the instant disposable animal. Chickens and ducks live for only seven weeks, piglets and turkeys for just a few months. The laying hen is fit only for stock-cubes after little more than a year in her cage. Worn-out breeding sows and dairy cows survive for only half as long as those on pre-war farms.

In the factory farm, some creatures are unable to survive for even these short periods. Picking out their bodies from the living mass can be a time-consuming task for the staff, so broiler-chicken producers usually leave them there to rot, and a machine is now being developed to help the battery-egg producer to locate the dead in the cages. But the majority of edible animals, sharing our tenacious instinct to survive, will succeed in doing so for their short designated lives. Only, however, with the aid of the antibiotics and mass medication which is now necessary to keep them alive in the conditions in which they are 'farmed'.

In all of us, humans, animals, even plants, the powerful

reproductive instinct survives the harshest situations. This is even more true of farm animals which have been selected and bred to be prolific. The battery hen lays her daily egg not because she is content, but because she is so strongly biologically programmed to do so that she cannot stop, however we treat her. And it is hard to see how we could treat her worse.

The factory farmer who seeks to convince us that modern production is based on kind treatment of animals is, I must confess, my personal *bête noire*. This is the chap who will never let you actually *see* those happy creatures, living their 'contented' lives. Fortunately, during the past years, I have met some better members of this breed, farmers who are frankly troubled by what they are doing and are wondering how to find a way out of the system: 'If God's a chicken, we're in trouble,' said one.

Indeed.

Now, along with everything else, the whole cost-saving basis of post-war agriculture is being questioned. Intensive units are tremendously expensive to build. Often, they only really paid off when we, the taxpayers, helped to foot the bill with huge subsidies. Now that these building subsidies have stopped, it is, for instance, proving more economical to set up free-range pig systems than to build more of the intensive units.

There are many other huge overheads involved in intensive farming: feeds, fuel, machinery, antibiotics and other medications all have to be bought, and chemicals to replace the natural replenishment of the land from animal and crop rotation. As EEC taxpayers, we pay out billions of pounds to buy and store the excess products of our factory farms. Nearly £20bn was forked out for this purpose by European taxpayers in 1989. Overall, farming subsidies have been costing each British family an estimated £17 a week in extra food bills and tax. No one has even begun to add up the cost to the environment.

Whether, when we take into account the real 'overheads', there is any saving to society in keeping animals in factories, rather than fields, is exceedingly doubtful. And for those still prone to fret about such things, there isn't even the comfort of 'food security'. Our present highly automated agriculture is now dependent on fossil fuel. Much easier to cut off, should those U-boats return to take another crack at us.

2. EXCLUSIVE INTERVIEWS WITH PIGS, HENS AND SHEEP

'**T**HE export of live horses for meat is outrageous,' a horse-owner complained on Radio 4 recently, rightly protesting against proposed 1992 changes in EEC regulations: 'After all, they aren't SHEEP!'

How comforting it must be for this genuine animal lover to believe that the half million live sheep exported from Britain each year are quite content to be crammed into lorries – sometimes more than four hundred in one vehicle – shaken, jolted, many of them injured, and deprived of food and water for long periods. And that they suffer less than horses would from such treatment.

However, he can hardly be blamed. We are encouraged to think of farm animals as something quite different from wild animals or those which we regard as friends or pets. Even British law makes a similar distinction, and we could be prosecuted for keeping our pets in the conditions permitted for farm animals. Surely farm animals are content to live in the ways that we have designed for them, knowing no better.

Or are they?

In the late 1970s, Professor David Wood-Gush and his colleagues of Edinburgh University's School of Agriculture began a fascinating five-year experiment by releasing a group of intensively reared pigs, the kind which supply our pork and bacon, on to an area of land on a slope of the Pentland Hills. The land provided them with a nicely varied habitat of woodland, stream and bog, as well as pasture. The pigs were given additional food to compensate for the limited area of their land, but were otherwise left to live naturally. They were then carefully observed over the following years.

One of the first things the pigs did was to set about building communal nests, in which groups of six to eight friends and relatives would later spend warm and cosy nights. Some of them brought grass and branches in their mouths from considerable distances to provide materials, while others built the nest walls and hollowed out beds.

The pigs lost no time in exploring and making full use of their environment, which kept them busily employed for most of each day. They learned how to use their snouts to lever out thick edible roots from the border of the forest, overturn grass tussocks to find worms, and locate such treats as resin. (Pigs have a sweet tooth!) Young grass was grazed with care to preserve the pasture. On warm days, the pigs regularly wallowed in boggy places or in the stream. At noon they took a siesta.

Their social behaviour was even more intriguing. The pigs helped each other to groom, greeted each other with friendly grunts and nose-rubs when waking in the morning and returning to their nest at night. As all pigs will do, if they have the chance, they even established communal 'loos', well away from the nests, rather than defecating in a haphazard way in the grass.

Aggression sometimes occurred when they competed for food, but generally they avoided this by spacing themselves out when foraging and grazing. Pregnant sows sought suitable sites, well away from the group's

home range, and built individual nests in which to give birth in peace and privacy.

In fact, Professor Wood-Gush concluded that within six months all these pigs were behaving in almost exactly the same way as their ancestor, the wild boar.

Many other scientists have now observed this same swift reversion to nature, not only by pigs but also by other 'domesticated' farm animals. Even before the Scottish study of pigs, domestic chickens, released on an island off Australia by Professor Glen McBride and colleagues were found to adapt quickly to the behaviour patterns of their own primitive ancestor, the red jungle fowl of Asia. They formed small social groups, raised and defended their broods, and roosted together in the trees at night. Factory-farmed ducks, artificially incubated and reared without sight of water (except to drink) are found to adapt just as quickly to a natural environment. Whether they are young birds or adult when they are released, they quickly take to swimming, diving for food and grazing on weeds. Like a duck to water!

Research now clearly reveals that farm animals are very little different from wild animals. One of the few ways in which they have changed is to be less disturbed by the close proximity of people; they are prepared to practise what natural behaviour is allowed them – breeding in particular – in the presence of man.

Otherwise, many centuries of 'domestication', even the totally unnatural confinement and breeding practices of the post-war decades, has not succeeded in eradicating their basic natural behaviour patterns.

In recent years, scientists have devised ingenious tests to reveal the animals' true natures and high degree of intelligence – and to allow these creatures, at last, to 'speak for themselves'.

Can a pig think? Yes, indeed, almost certainly as well as, or better than, a dog. A wide range of intelligence tests have shown that farm animals can quickly learn to complete difficult tasks, such as finding their way out of mazes, and operating complex machinery to turn up the heating when they feel chilly. Such tests suggest that cattle, sheep and goats, as well as pigs, are at least as intelligent as dogs. And probably more intelligent than horses!

Due to our own lack of understanding, their apparent passivity is sometimes wrongly interpreted as stupidity. Sheep, for instance, have a vested interest in not showing pain. When attacked by predators they cannot, unlike some other species, count on help from fellow members of the flock. And a predator is likely to be encouraged if its victim appears to be wounded. So a sheep's best tactic is to hide its pain. Thus, when tagged at auctions by having large holes punched through their ears – an unnecessary cruelty which occurs daily – they show little or no reaction.

Grazing animals may appear to lead uncomplicated lives but the truth is quite the reverse. Sheep and cattle must learn which of many different plants they should eat and which not. They identify patches of good pasture and they work out how long the grass will take to regrow after grazing, for they do not return until the energy to be gained from eating the grass will outweigh the energy expended in getting there. Quite a complex equation that would be well beyond my maths. But not those of a sheep.

All farm animals are highly inquisitive, and their desire for stimuli, diversion and exploration is so strong that, in some studies, it has proved even greater than their desire for food.

They require considerable intelligence for the complex task of establishing and maintaining relationships. Pigs, cattle, sheep and poultry rely on their flock or herd for security, comfort, information, help in grooming and many other things. Note how startled grazing animals group together to run. Or the panic of a single sheep when your path through a field separates it from the flock.

The social interaction of animals is now recognized by scientists as a manifestation of their conscious choice and need of company. To keep veal calves or pigs in isolation, as is now common, is, in itself, a profound cruelty.

Within the herd or flock, farm animals, given the freedom to do so, form subgroups, reminiscent of our own society. Family groups, swaggering groups of young bachelors (we know the type!), play groups of young lambs or pigs. And within these subgroups are pairs of friends.

Scientists have long known that farm animals form friendships, deliberately choosing the regular company of another animal. Sometimes such friends will have been reared together, but often the attachment will have been formed later in life. Cattle friends often groom each other, and always graze close together. As do sheep friends, which are particularly easy to spot among widely dispersed hill flocks. But you can spot such pairs in any field of sheep. These animals take care to position themselves, while grazing, at an angle which allows them to stay reassuringly in sight of one another.

Of course there are bosses and middle-management in the animal world, as in all societies. The famous 'pecking order'. But the idea that this order results from aggression is now outdated.

The social order is, in fact, much more complex. There are 'leaders', who are always at the front when the group moves, but the timing and direction of movement may be determined by other individuals who are 'controllers' of group activity. Neither leader nor controller need be the strongest individual. In many cases, individuals in a social group will each regularly undertake a different task. Such is the sophistication of their social order that when dairy cows organize themselves to enter the milking shed, high-yielding cows are given an advanced position in the queue.

Dominant animals have probably been aggressive, in the past, in order to achieve their positions. But when animals live in suitable conditions and established groups there is rarely cause for this.

'Avoidance behaviour is the key factor which achieves social harmony,' explains the eminent animal-behaviour expert, Professor Donald Broom, of Cambridge University. 'There are many subtle animal gestures which cut out conflict.'

A tilt of the head by a submissive pig or sheep acts like the cap-doffing of the old farm-hand to the boss. Similarly, a lift of the head and a long hard gaze from the boss – be he pig or man – acts as an unmistakable signal to any sensible subordinate.

However, such communication can only bring harmony if the environment is satisfactory: each animal must be able to recognize all of its flock mates and must

have enough space to be able to get out of the way when necessary. Cattle are thought to be able to remember up to seventy herd mates, pigs up to thirty, hens – where evidence is less clear – possibly only ten, but maybe up to a hundred members of a flock.

In factory farms animals are crammed together in hundreds of thousands, in hysteria-inducing conditions in which there is no space for avoidance or any other conflict-reducing behaviour. Then factory farmers complain about the 'vices' of their animals.

Scientists have made detailed studies of how animals react to modern intensive systems. They have learned, for instance, how sows, whose natural behaviour is to spend the day busily employed, occupy their time when confined – as so many still are – in metal-barred stalls little bigger than their own bodies or tethered on short chains.

One popular pastime among these sows is bar biting. The sow mouths the bar across the front of the stall – often repeatedly moving her head from side to side. Some animals even injure themselves by repeated movements which involve bumping their heads.

Sham chewing is also common. It passes the time! With nothing in their mouths but saliva, pigs spend lengthy periods chewing vigorously, their mouths froth-ing. Sham chewing can occupy a pig for as much as half a day. Chain biting is another example of stereotyped behaviour which has been reported by Professor Broom and his colleagues.

Does this sound, to you, like a contented adjustment to a different way of life? Or, as one scientist concluded on this evidence, as more like 'animals showing signs resembling those of human psychiatric disorders'.

Animals are subject to clinical depression. The apathy (a key symptom in human depression) displayed by long-confined sows, and their unnatural lack of reaction to attempts to stimulate them, suggests that they may well be suffering from this condition.

The behavioural needs of farm animals have now been so well researched that scientists can even determine the degree and relative importance of these needs: for in-stance, whether company counts for more than space to an animal (it often does!) and whether a hen needs the seclusion of a nest for egg-laying so much that she will face what, to her, are fearful situations in order to reach it (she will!).

Such considerations have been totally, completely and utterly ignored in devising the systems which still pre-dominate in factory farming. The animals' needs were simply not taken into account. All that mattered to the politicians and the factory farmers was the cost. Now, as some farmers are starting to return to systems which treat animals as the intelligent sensitive creatures they are – not as machines – it is up to us. At last we consumers can choose whether the meat and eggs that we buy are factory-farmed or not. Will we too allow cost to be the only deciding factor?

3. A MESSAGE FROM GOD
TO JOHN GUMMER

ALMOST invariably, in any discussion with a factory farmer, there comes a moment when he is prepared to concede a little ground. Well, yes, perhaps life isn't ideal for all of today's farmed animals, he will admit. Certainly, it isn't as good as *he* himself would like to see it. (He has, of course, already established that he is a devoted animal lover. Does he not own a dog?) Now he fixes you with a look which leaves no doubt that he also remembers his mother's birthday, uses environmentally friendly toilet paper and cares deeply for the poor. 'But after all,' he announces with sad finality, 'people *MUST* have cheap meat.'

So deeply entrenched is his belief that there is often a silence when you ask: 'Why?'

How remarkable it is that agribusinessmen, and the politicians who support them, have succeeded in remaining unaware of so much scientific evidence in recent years. Evidence which clearly indicates that our large intake of 'unnatural' animal foods, at the expense of plant foods, is one of the major causes of serious illness in our society.

Health experts repeatedly appeal to us to eat less of the former and more of the latter. But, as one of our most eminent nutritionists, Professor Philip James, recently remarked: 'British agricultural policy takes no account at all of the present British nutritional policy.' Loyally, it continues to adhere to the mistaken nutritional beliefs of half a century ago.

Ministers of Agriculture, dedicated to supporting the agricultural status quo, have simply ignored modern health policy when – as so often happens – the two conflict. The following sequence of events illustrates this.

MAY 1990   Minister of Agriculture, Fisheries and Food, John Gummer, warmly applauded by an audience of meat traders, attacked vegetarians as 'deeply undemocratic food faddists'. He was reported, in *The Times*, as saying that vegetarianism was a 'wholly unnatural practice' and that he was tired of reading about the 10 per cent of the population who had turned vegetarian or reduced their meat intake.

JUNE 1990   A diet survey conducted by his own department and the Department of Health revealed that over 85 per cent of British adults were consuming more fat than is recommended by government health authorities, and that 65 per cent had over-high cholesterol levels. Their major source of cholesterol-raising fat was revealed to be – meat and meat dishes.

Such conflict between agricultural and nutritional policy adds further to the confusion of the consumer, who is already profoundly confused. And with good cause. Were not the middle-aged among us brought up to believe that large quantities of meat, milk, cheese and eggs were exceedingly good for us? We were. Now we are told by all health authorities (though not, of course, by the Minister of Agriculture) that such excess is exceedingly bad for us.

Nutritional advice in the immediate post-war era stemmed from a suspicion that protein deficiency might be the key factor in causing malnutrition. This ignited a mighty bonfire of belief in this 'miracle nutrient'. And, at that time, protein meant, essentially, animal protein. It was not known then, as it is now, that mixed protein from cereals and vegetables is generally every bit as valuable.

The nutritionists, although with the best of intentions, had made a mistake. The real problem was not protein deficiency, but insufficient calorie intake resulting from poverty.

It is now known that it is exceedingly difficult to go short of protein. Not impossible, of course. I must caution those banana eaters of Uganda and taro eaters of New Guinea who are among my readers, on that score. There, where food is in short supply, variety severely limited and the staple food itself particularly low in protein, the body may not be able to obtain its daily protein requirement. The rest of us, as long as we aren't going hungry, can afford to feel pretty relaxed about it.

Generally, even those in the poorest Third World countries, eating no animal food at all, are found to get sufficient protein so long as they get sufficient calories.

Nutritionists are even beginning to suspect (something unthinkable a few years ago) that too much protein could be bad for us. Until recently, it was the saturated fat content of the modern animal-rich diet which was pinpointed as the cause of most ills. But such a diet is also particularly high in protein. Perhaps too high. Strong evidence has now emerged of the adverse effects of excess protein intake on the kidneys, and some recent studies suggest that this may also be a factor in the development of cancer and of osteoporosis, the brittle-bone condition which now afflicts so many post-menopausal women in Western society.

As research proceeds, this once sainted nutrient may, like so many other nutrients, be exposed as a considerable sinner when consumed in excess.

Meanwhile, Mr Gummer, who quoted the Bible in his attack on vegetarians, attempting to enlist even the Almighty in his pro-meat lobby, may be particularly interested to know that God's RDA (recommended daily allowance) for protein works out at half that currently advised by Britain's health authorities. In human mother's milk, He provides only 5 per cent of the calories in the form of protein: British adults, who need less protein than fast-growing youngsters, are advised that they should consume 10 per cent.

Protein is scattered so widely in everything that grows that it is hard even for vegans, on a varied diet, to consume less than the healthy minimum. The divine intent appears to be that, like the lilies of the field, we simply shouldn't have to worry about getting all we need. But then poor old God lacks the mighty multi-national-company promotion budgets that in so many ways (research funds, advertising, public relations, etc.) sustain the idea of high protein need – and our present unnatural and possibly dangerous excess of it.

As well as factory farmers, companies who supply chemicals, machinery and animal feeds such as cereals and soya beans also have a major vested interest in sustaining our high intake of animal products (you sell more cereal or soya if you recycle it through animals, since much is wasted in food conversion). No company makes money from persuading us to eat less. The 'politics of protein' is a phrase familiar to every nutritionist who has done battle in the international power arena.

But, when the protein myth began, the nation was encouraged to go to work on an egg, ideally two, to tuck into steak, chops and cheese, and to wash it all down with great pints of full-cream milk, in the genuine belief that you couldn't get too much of this particular good thing.

As a result, we and other affluent nations embarked on an experiment with our health quite amazing in its audacity when you sit back and think about it. And it is well worth doing so.

Nutrition is a relatively new science and very little is yet known of the ways in which the many complex substances in food affect the human body. The body itself is equally complex. Where the chain reactions that are triggered off by various changes are concerned, there is much that still remains a mystery to medicine. It takes hundreds of generations for selective adaptation to take place in response to a change in diet. So, radical change in anything so fundamental to our well-being seems risky, to say the least.

Clearly it is wise to consider what manner of diet has enabled man to survive, successfully, for so many millennia. Here we hit a clamour of conflict. 'Man is by nature a herbivore,' shout one lot, citing societies where this was so. 'Oh no he's not, he's a natural omnivore,' come cries from the opposing camp. Possibly the latter have even more evidence to support them. But on one fact every expert is agreed: the diet of today's Western omnivore has little similarity to that of his prehistoric ancestor. Nor even to that of his pre-war Grampa!

We have hugely increased our intake of animal products. At the same time we have greatly altered the nature of these products.

Our nearest relative, the chimpanzee, provides perhaps the strongest clue to man's natural diet. The chimp lives predominantly on plants, but is not a vegan. Occasionally he will kill and eat small monkeys, steal birds' eggs, even kill the birds when he can catch them. He has developed an ingenious habit of poking a stick into an ant's nest and then sucking the ants off this tasty 'lollipop'. But all such animal additions to his diet come into the category of occasional treats. As, it seems, did such foods for man throughout the centuries.

Certainly, in recent centuries, many of the rich stuffed themselves with meat. Henry VIII was thought to live on little else, and that, you may recall from reading recent scientific theory, is what is now thought to have finished him off. But for the majority, animal foods were eaten in quantity only on festive occasions. There are even some alive today (I name no names) who are old enough to recall the days when a chicken was a special treat.

Indeed, although it pains me to draw attention to the fact, the 'wholly unnatural practice' followed by Mr Gummer's vegetarian 'food faddists' corresponds much more closely to man's natural eating pattern than do the eating practices of Mr Gummer. Though vegetarian diets vary (some eat dairy products, others dairy products and eggs), the majority obtain most of their food from plants and a smaller proportion from animals. As have most men throughout history.

This could well be why Western vegetarians run only about a third of the risk of getting coronary heart disease and a considerably lower risk of suffering from several common cancers than do the rest of the population. On

their more natural diets cholesterol and blood-pressure levels are lower and their health is generally better than that of the rest of us.

It was only with the advent of factory farming that animal food became our major source of calories. And, in crowding the animals indoors and feeding them on man-determined diets, we completed a process that significantly altered the nature of most of these foods.

The wild animals hunted by primitive hunter-gatherers had very little body fat, and what they had was largely of the unsaturated kind – now considered beneficial to our health. In domesticating animals we chose those species, sheep, cattle, goats and pigs, which have a higher natural content of saturated fat. Then we increased the quantity of such fat by selective breeding.

In bringing farm animals into factories we took the denaturalization process a stage further. How an animal lives and eats plays a large part in determining the nature of its fat. The farmyard chicken of old was able to exercise and to supplement its diet by pecking around at plants, insects, worms, etc. This would tend to give it low overall fat content, and to cause a higher proportion of its fat to be unsaturated. Today's indoor broiler has no such opportunities. And substances in the concentrates it is fed, in many cases, shift the balance still further towards saturated fats. The figures generally given for a chicken's fat content stem from analysis made more than a decade ago. There may be some nasty shocks when the work is updated.

Increasingly, we are becoming aware of the link between the unnatural feeding and rearing of farm animals and dangerous food. BSE, 'mad cow disease', is just one such example. Worryingly high levels of chemicals have recently been found in some farmed fish. Now pregnant women are advised not to eat liver because of its sometimes dangerously high vitamin A content.

When more is known, the changes we have made to animals through our modern agricultural methods may well prove to have been even more dangerous than the over-high quantity of animal food we consume. It is significant that fish, mainly swimming freely and choosing their own diet, are the only animal food that health experts now recommend us to eat in increased quantity.

Many people who are aware of the links between food and health now choose only fish and those animal foods of lower fat content. This has some virtue. But unless they also reduce their total intake of animal food and eat a higher proportion of cereal, fruit and vegetables, they are only half right. They ignore not only today's diet guidelines but also the natural diet of our ancestors.

Schooled on the idea of eating 'an apple a day to keep the doctor away', we have little notion of the quantity of fruit, vegetables and cereals that a natural healthy diet requires.

An apple?

Some years ago a British anthropologist spent some time in Tanzania studying a tribe which was believed to have behaviour patterns similar to those of primitive man. He went there to study their strange language but found himself equally intrigued by their strange diet. Although their diet included some meat, they consumed berries, when they came across them, in amazing quantities. Whole bushes and trees were stripped of what looked like ripe hawthorn berries. Individuals would each consume many pounds in one go.

Needing more calories than modern man to fuel his more energetic life, and with meat less easily available, primitive man must have consumed a very large amount of low-calorie plants. And with them, vast quantities of substances such as vitamin C, B-carotene, other plant pigments and dietary fibre.

As you will see at the end of this chapter, much evidence is now emerging that such plant substances help to protect us against our most serious modern Western ailments; and that other substances, consumed in excess, in foods of animal origin, may help to cause these ailments.

Do vegetarians owe their better health to a plentiful intake of these protective substances? Or, is it largely due to the fact that, by restricting their animal food intake, they avoid large quantities of harmful substances? Or, is it, as seems likely in the present state of knowledge, a combination of the two factors?

I have not yet mentioned such risks as food poisoning, salmonella, etc., which have occupied acres of newsprint of late, and I do not intend to discuss these problems in any detail, in the interest of tree preservation. Clearly, however, it is high time that those 'Now wash your hands' notices were taken down from lavatory walls and stuck on to chickens. Most of us have already mastered our toilet training. But many people still remain unaware that a large proportion of uncooked chickens are now

infected with potentially harmful bacteria, and touching them – without careful hand-washing afterwards – is a health hazard.

There are many other ways in which today's unnatural feeding and rearing of animals puts health at risk. But, for most of us, the increasing evidence that our diet is the major cause of coronaries and cancers gives the greatest cause for concern. Which is why those of us with even a modicum of understanding of modern nutrition are trying to move our eating practices nearer to those of the enviably healthy vegetarians, and worrying, in our caring way, about those who seem less able to understand the clear messages of science.

As one nutritionist put it: 'The evidence may not always be conclusive, but the signposts are clear and numerous, and every one of them points in the same direction.'

Would somebody, please, tell John Selwyn Gummer.

THE STAY-ALIVE GUIDE

LONG gone, in the West, are the days when contracting a serious illness was simply a matter of bad luck. Such infective ailments as TB, polio, diphtheria and cholera are largely conquered. But in their place we have degenerative ailments such as coronaries and cancers, believed to arise, over long periods, from the way we live today. In particular, from the way in which we eat. It is now suspected that the process which leads to such illnesses frequently starts as early as childhood.

Coronary heart disease is now the major cause of death in Britain and our death rates from it are among the highest in the world. Cancer comes second, and accounts for 23 per cent of all deaths, with lung, breast and large-bowel cancers among the most common. Although about a third of all cancer deaths are attributable to smoking, an even higher proportion (35 per cent) have been estimated by one of the world's leading experts, Professor Sir Richard Doll, to be related to diet.

Dietary clues about what causes such illnesses and what protects us against them have been emerging at an increasing rate over recent years. In some instances, the scientific evidence is strong. In others it at least deserves to be taken seriously.

Almost invariably, it is the plant foods which appear

to be protective and the animal foods, eaten in the present excess, which appear to be causative.

Nutritionists know, from many studies, which plant foods are beneficial. At present, however, they can only surmise which nutrients in these foods are responsible. But it could be other substances, or a combination of nutrients. So there is no easy alternative protection to be found from vitamin pills – although these have their value in some other respects.

I have only referred to some of the most serious illnesses in compiling the guide on the following pages. If the threat of cancer isn't enough to give you cause for serious thought about your diet, I doubt whether kidney stones or constipation will.

CORONARY HEART DISEASE

One in twelve men in Britain die prematurely (before the age of sixty-five) from this cause.

BELIEVED TO BE CAUSATIVE
Animal fats (eggs and other cholesterol-rich foods in some cases)

A vast quantity of scientific evidence shows that a high intake of fat – in particular of the saturated fat supplied by meat and dairy products – is a major cause of heart attacks. Saturated fat raises the level of cholesterol in the blood. This can cause blockages in the arteries, cutting off the blood supply to the heart. For some people (usually those whose parents have died young from heart attacks) dietary cholesterol itself, richly supplied in egg yolks and offal, can be a risk factor. But for most it is the quantity of animal fat consumed and also smoking which constitute the major risk factors.

BELIEVED TO BE PROTECTIVE
Oily sea fish (salmon, herrings, mackerel, sardines, pilchards)
Oats
Beans

There is strong evidence that the oils provided by oily sea fish are protective against heart disease. Diets rich in cereal, fruit and vegetables have also generally emerged as being protective, in many studies, and oats and beans can play some part in helping to lower blood cholesterol levels.

FOOD FOR THOUGHT

Non-vegetarians in Western societies are three times more likely to die from coronary heart disease than vegetarians. A number of studies suggest that the protective effect of a vegetarian diet is proportionately related to the degree of vegetarianism practised. Vegans, i.e. those who do not even consume eggs or dairy products, run only a tenth of the risk of heart attacks of omnivores, while ordinary vegetarians experience a greater protective effect than do those who eat meat occasionally.

BREAST CANCER

This is the most common form of cancer among women in Britain, and the incidence is increasing.

BELIEVED TO BE CAUSATIVE
Animal fats (milk fat in particular)
Alcohol

A high consumption of fat has been widely cited as being important in the development of breast cancer. Studies in the United States have found that this type of cancer correlates more closely with the consumption

of milk fat than with any other type of fat. Some research has also suggested that a high or even moderate consumption of alcohol may also be a causative factor.

BELIEVED TO BE PROTECTIVE
Fruit and vegetables in general

Although lowering fat intake is the main dietary recommendation for the prevention of breast cancer, there is some evidence that carotene and vitamins C and E could be protective. Since these nutrients are all provided by plant foods, medical committees have recommended an increased intake of cereals, fruit and vegetables as a protective measure against breast cancer.

FOOD FOR THOUGHT

Populations consuming high levels of fat and animal protein have the highest breast-cancer mortality rates. This illness is uncommon in countries where the diet is mainly vegetarian. Sir Richard Doll believes that 'Diet may have a substantial effect on the incidence of breast cancer – certainly enough to be concerned about.'

LUNG CANCER

BELIEVED TO BE CAUSATIVE
No known dietary cause

Smoking is by far the commonest cause of this illness and is responsible for 95 per cent of lung cancers in men and 85 per cent in women in this country. There are no known dietary causes.

BELIEVED TO BE PROTECTIVE
Carrots
Broccoli
Spinach
Spring greens
Spring cabbage
Watercress

Many population and animal studies indicate that carrots and dark-green leafy vegetables (broccoli, spinach, spring greens, spring cabbage, watercress) have a protective effect against lung cancer. There is a substantial weight of evidence in this instance. B-carotene, found in high concentration in the vegetables listed, has been thought to be responsible, but it could prove to be some other as yet unidentified constituent. It appears that the protective substance in these vegetables acts as a 'scavenger' of the loose oxygen in the tissue which can convert harmless substances into noxious ones.

FOOD FOR THOUGHT

Even smokers with a high consumption of these protective vegetables appear less likely to contract lung cancer than those with lower intake. It must be emphasized, however, that smoking is by far the greatest risk factor. Diet plays a very secondary role in the development of this disease.

CANCER OF THE PROSTATE

This accounts for about 10 per cent of cancer deaths in men.

BELIEVED TO BE CAUSATIVE
Animal fats

Studies have shown that the incidence of cancer of the prostate is higher among men consuming a large quantity of animal fats.

BELIEVED TO BE PROTECTIVE
Possibly vegetables

Nothing specific has emerged here, but again there are indications that substances in vegetables may be protective.

FOOD FOR THOUGHT

Overweight men are more at risk of contracting cancer of the prostate than those who are slim. Vegetarians are less prone to excess weight than omnivores.

LARGE-BOWEL CANCERS

(Cancers of the colon, rectum and bowel)

BELIEVED TO BE CAUSATIVE
Animal fat
Possibly meat protein

There is a large amount of evidence indicating that a high intake of animal fat is a risk factor, as with most other forms of cancer. Some studies also suggest that a high intake of meat, and possibly animal protein, may increase the risk. It could be a combination of the two factors.

BELIEVED TO BE PROTECTIVE
Dried beans
Chick-peas

Root vegetables
Bananas
Wholegrain wheat
Rye
Cauliflower
Cabbage
Broccoli
Brussels sprouts

Substances found in two groups of plant foods are thought to be protective, in different ways, against these forms of cancer. The benefits of dietary fibre in bulking out the faeces and facilitating the easy, speedy elimination of waste matter are well known. New research now suggests that some of the starch, as well as fibre, in cereals and vegetables remains undigested in the small intestine and contributes to this effect. Indeed, it may well be the major factor. The type of beans which are dried, such as red kidney beans, and also chick-peas, are rich sources of this 'resistant starch', as well as of dietary fibre, and are thought to be of particular protective value. Bananas, potatoes and other root vegetables also appear to supply useful quantities of 'resistant starch' and wholegrain wheat and rye supply beneficial fibre.

Other studies have shown that the cruciferous family of vegetables (which are named for their four-petalled flowers – cauliflower, cabbage, broccoli and Brussels sprouts) contain other substances which inhibit the production of large-bowel cancers by a different mechanism.

FOOD FOR THOUGHT

Population studies have shown a strong correlation between the consumption of fat and meat per capita and the incidence of large-bowel cancers. The greater the intake of the former, the greater the incidence of the latter.

The American National Cancer Institute estimates that the incidence of colon cancer could be reduced by 50 per cent through dietary changes.

CANCER OF THE STOMACH

This is one of the few cancers which have declined in incidence in the West since the early decades of this century. From being one of the most common it has become quite rare.

BELIEVED TO BE CAUSATIVE
Salt-preserved foods

Salting was the most common method of preserving food until this century, and salt-preserved food is thought to have been the major cause of stomach cancer. It may not necessarily have been the salt itself which caused this cancer, and better methods of preserving, especially refrigeration, could be the important factor.

BELIEVED TO BE PROTECTIVE
Vitamin-C-rich fruit (citrus) and vegetables

There is strong evidence that vitamin C is the main protective factor. This is richly supplied by citrus fruits, now more widely available all the year round, as are fresh and frozen vegetables, which also supply vitamin C.

FOOD FOR THOUGHT

There is strong evidence that dietary factors were the main cause of this cancer and that dietary changes are the main reason for its present rarity in Britain.

4. FOUR HUNDRED MILLION FURTHER REASONS FOR EATING LESS MEAT

PERHAPS the real concern motivating our factory farmer to cram still more chickens, turkeys, calves or pigs into his intensive units is not our own overfed population, but the four hundred million underfed people of the Third World? It would in fact be difficult to find a more effective way to rob them of what little food they have, since our over-consumption of animal products is one of the major causes of Third World starvation. Link after link, it makes up a chain of ills which encircles the world.

There is enough food grown in the world today to feed everyone. About that there is no dispute. Even the grain alone is sufficient to provide everyone in the world with 3,000 calories daily, enough to make many of us fat. Hunger is caused by the way in which this food is shared out. Much more of it ends up in the affluent West than in the Third World.

One of the main reasons for this is the vast waste involved in recycling such a large proportion of the world's crops through animals. In producing meat, dairy products or eggs we lose 80–90 per cent of the calories which would have been supplied by the crops if we ate them directly in the form of cereal or vegetable foods. Animals consume many more calories than they eventually provide in the form of meat, eggs or milk.

Of course, some areas of land, such as our own uplands, are unsuitable for crop growing. Grazing animals there, or elsewhere as part of traditional (or organic) rotation, which keeps the land in good health, need not drain the world of food. Similarly, some parts of plants, not edible for humans, can supplement the animals' winter food. But such a sensible use of food resources would not permit us to continue our present massive – and unhealthy – over-consumption of animal products.

More than 40 per cent of the world's grain is now fed to animals. In addition, vast areas of land are devoted to the growth of other animal-feed crops, such as soya beans. Each year the world's cattle alone consume enough food to satisfy the calorific needs of almost double the world's present human population.

To satisfy the huge demand for animal feed in Europe, we import large quantities of crops grown in the poorest Third World countries. Their governments are eager to grow and export these 'cash crops' in an attempt to reduce their massive debts. The rich and powerful people of such countries often benefit greatly from this trade; the effect on the poor, the great mass of the population, is, in most cases, quite the reverse.

Many years ago, while travelling in Kenya, I met an Englishman who told me why he had chosen a career as an agricultural engineer. As an idealistic young man it had seemed to him the best way to help the hungry of the world. Older, wiser and now much-travelled, he had witnessed the disastrous consequences of so many of the well-meant schemes he had helped to develop. Huge agricultural machines, bought with borrowed cash or given as aid, had displaced the peasants who worked in the fields, thus adding them to the swelling throngs of hungry people in the cities. The poor grew poorer. Only a tiny land-owning minority grew rich.

This is the common result of 'cash-crop' exports from the Third World. Sometimes 'the rich' are multinational companies who buy or lease the best of the land. Land prices rise. The poor must struggle to scratch a living from land hardly capable of sustaining them. This, in turn, contributes to one of the most massive environmental problems afflicting the world today: soil erosion.

Every year, an area of the world as large as England and Scotland combined becomes infertile. There are a number of causes of soil erosion and desertification, many of them linked with our over-consumption of animal products. The spread of cattle ranches which produce beef for export is the main reason why the tropical rainforests are being felled at today's alarming rate. Once robbed of its protective cover of trees, the shallow soil in these areas is cracked in the hot sun and then washed away by torrential rain. Within a few years, little will remain and it will not be capable of feeding anything.

Soil erosion is by no means confined to the Third World. In America, where every sandwich seems to contain half a turkey or the side of a cow, billions of dollars have been poured into efforts to stem the erosion problem caused by their intensive post-war agriculture. And still it gets worse. Over four million acres of their crop land are lost to soil erosion each year.

Those of us who garden with passion could tell them why. Which of us would dream of treating our herbaceous borders only with chemical fertilizers, which feed the plants but do not replenish the soil? In autumn, we apply many wheelbarrow-loads of compost and manure, since the soil must be properly fed. We take care of this in our gardens. Not, however, in many of the fields.

Which is why, even in Britain, in a temperate maritime climate, which is least likely to give rise to this problem, soil erosion has started to cause serious concern in many areas.

But while the soil grows thin from the lack of organic matter, huge quantities of manure accumulate at factory farms. Why, you may sensibly inquire, is it not used to replenish the soil?

Loading, transporting and spreading livestock wastes is a costly business. It is simply not economically viable to transport manure over distances of more than eight miles. And, these days, most crops are grown in one part of the country while the animals are kept in another.

Where factory-farmed animals are deprived of straw bedding, as so many are, their excrement ends up as a semi-liquid slurry. Frequently this slurry, many times more polluting than human sewage, seeps out of the lagoons in which it is kept and enters our rivers. Intensive farming of pigs and cattle is now one of Britain's major causes of water pollution and the destruction of wildlife in the rivers.

On and on goes the chain-reaction of destruction. Intensive farming is even destroying the beauty of the British countryside: hedgerows which have existed for centuries to contain the grazing animals are ripped out and the wildlife which they supported disappears. Add this loss and the overfishing of the seas (much of it to supply fishmeal for animal feed) to world starvation, desertification, pollution, the suffering of millions of animals and the serious damage to human health and you begin to get a picture of the consequences of our present intensive methods of agriculture.

You may even reach the conclusion that it is not entirely a good thing.

5. PLEASE DON'T TRY TOO HARD

Let's be fair – during the post-war years the factory farmers have, as they often point out, done exactly what we asked of them. They have supplied masses of the cheap animal products once so mistakenly thought to do us good. And how tactfully they have sustained the soothing pastoral image of the old-fashioned farm in their advertising and kept their factory doors locked, catering to our sensitive desire not to know of the horrors going on inside.

Perhaps our ostrich attitude stemmed largely from the fact that it was not easy for us to do anything to help to stop factory farming. Eating habits are hard to change. Many of us do not find it easy to become vegetarian. Short of that, it was rather hard to know what we could do to help.

Now, at last, the easy answers have started to arrive. They are sitting there on the shelves of local supermarkets and stores: new, healthier and more kindly produced ranges of animal products which can open the door to a new era. All it needs is a gentle push from us.

On learning how badly so many animals are treated, I hope you will resolve never again to buy anything other than the kinder alternatives recommended in this book. Well, *almost* never! I counsel against perfectionism in the light of my previous incarnation as a slimming expert. Over-determined diet bids often collapse completely on the consumption of a single wine-gum. So, the week after next, as you dash through Safeway's with something else on your mind and succumb, perhaps, to a suspect sandwich (was that a free-range egg?), do not, I beg you, abandon your new resolve in an aftermath of guilt.

Millions of us doing our best – making it clear by what we buy that we don't want cruelly produced products – can do even more than the admirable dedicated few to change the system. Every time you buy a 'kind alternative', you are doing something to put a stop to this appalling era of animal cruelty.

The supermarkets now sell such a large proportion of all animal products that they can largely dictate the methods by which animals are farmed. They will supply precisely what you and I, their customers, desire, and they will know what we want by what we buy. It's as simple as that.

Although kinder products cost more at present, we do not have to spend more on food overall if we also resolve to eat fewer animal products – as we should. Frankly, you have to be out of your mind not to reduce your intake on today's medical evidence.

Only kamikaze eaters now have bacon, eggs, etc., for breakfast; but when you start to add up the butter, milk, cheese, yoghurt and eggs, as well as the meat and poultry you eat in the course of a day, you will probably find that you and your family are consuming far more animal products than you realized.

There are several strategies for cutting down. One, which could prove effective in habit-changing, would be a policy of having one completely animal-product-free meal each day. Perhaps a vegan lunch. Or, alternatively, you could have one or two strict vegetarian days each week. Another way is simply to use animal products, as leading nutritionist Dr David Southgate advises, as a 'garnish' to each meal, not its focus. A few prawns or anchovy fillets or a sprinkling of cheese on an otherwise vegetable-, pasta- or rice-based meal.

Such policies do not require the consumption of odd-sounding substances like 'tofu'. Remember, so long as we are getting sufficient calories from varied sources, we will be getting sufficient *protein* – probably more than enough – even if (as the health experts now so strongly recommend) the bulk of that food comes from cereal and vegetable sources.

If you are over forty, forget everything you learned about nutrition as a child. Most of it was wrong. Only the idea of obtaining food from a variety of sources remains valid – but, these days, this means that we should eat a wide variety of fruit, vegetables, pasta, rice, pulses and cereals.

Fling out all the outdated notions about meals. Instead of thinking of 'salad with —' (eggs, cheese, etc.), take advantage of the rich variety of vegetable exotica on every delicatessen counter to make the all-salad salad a satisfying meal. Very different from the dark green, limp lettuce, tomato, cucumber and little else of my own salad days.

Get out of a rut. Try, for a change, using recipes from vegetarian cookery books. Or sample some of those 'suitable for vegetarians' ready-meals which are an expanding feature of the supermarkets and shops.

In our household this demi-veg approach has added many interesting new dishes to the repertoire and cheered it up no end. I have discovered some marvellous vegetarian curries at a local delicatessen and a wide range of goodies at M & S, and I have learned to cook some inexpensive vegetarian dishes too. But you can't win

them all, so don't throw in the towel if the first vegetarian dish you try brings back painful memories of Woolton pie. It takes time to learn the tricks.

Another thing I have learned from studying eating behaviour is that we are often deceived in our yearnings for a particular food; many a pork pie, for instance, is eaten entirely in response to the desire for a big dollop of Branston pickle. So if you fry up the onions (in vegetable oil), pile on the relish and toast the bun, nobody will probably care much whether what goes inside is beef-burger or vegeburger.

Your kind-eating choices can largely determine the future of farming. But there are many powerful multinational companies with a vested interest in sustaining the present intensive system, with all its cruelties, so you might want to do even more to help.

If so, I recommend that you join the excellent and highly respected organization, Compassion in World Farming. I am a member, as are Joanna Lumley, Sir Richard Body, former chairman of the House of Commons Agricultural Committee, and John Baker, the present Bishop of Salisbury. None of us would quite come into the category of teenage terrorists. However, we share this organization's view that the least we owe to farm animals is a decent life and humane death.

To join us, all you have to do is send your name, address and the £10 annual membership subscription to: Compassion in World Farming, 20 Lavant Street, Petersfield, Hants GU32 3UW. In return they will send you a magazine several times a year, to tell you how you can help, with petitions, letters, leaflets, etc. At present, along with the RSPCA, this organization is campaigning against the cruel and totally unnecessary practice of exporting farm animals live to be slaughtered overseas.

The RSPCA is currently working on an excellent plan to improve conditions for farm animals. They have commissioned scientists and vets to develop kinder farming systems based on the needs of the animals. Producers agreeing to follow their guidelines (and to regular inspection) will be allowed to use a 'Freedom Food' logo – so please support these foods when they appear in the shops. And please recommend *The Kind Food Guide* to your friends. The animals need all the help they can get.

Never underestimate the power of letters either. Members of Parliament largely judge the importance of an issue to the public on the volume of their mail. Supermarkets admit that the large number of letters from their customers was in part responsible for the introduction of 'kinder lines'. Do not be put off if you are a rotten speller and a lousy letter-writer. All that matters is the volume of mail from nice, sensible-sounding people.

Farm animals can't write or speak, and, hidden away in their dark sheds they can't even show their suffering to the world. This is why they have become the 'untouchables', the weakest of the weak, the most cruelly abused of the suffering in our Western world. One day, I believe, we shall look back on this age and our treatment of animals with shame. Meanwhile, they need your help. God bless you, dear reader, on their behalf, for any help you are prepared to give.

PART TWO

GUIDE TO THE KINDER ALTERNATIVES

GUIDE TO THE KINDER ALTERNATIVES

TODAY's shopper has an advantage that hardly existed even a year ago: an easy opportunity to choose food from more humane and healthy systems of farming. Such foods have been available for some time for those prepared to seek them out – from organic farms, specialist butchers and home-delivery services. With their arrival in the supermarkets they gain a new accessibility. And with it the chance to come in from the fringe, gain popularity and change the face of farming.

Make no mistake: how farm animals are kept in the future depends on you. Will shoppers still go on choosing their chops and chicken for cheapness? If so, pigs will stay in chains and chickens in the horrendous broiler-houses. And shoppers deserve to run the health risks which are only beginning to be revealed. Or will you, as I'm sure you will, as a reader of this book, swell the growing number of those who now require to be reassured about how that animal was reared before they buy any meat or animal product?

In the third part of this book I have compiled a directory of information on every edible animal – fish, flesh and fowl – and on those producing eggs and milk, so that you can make an informed decision about which foods are healthy and humane. (The two factors so often go together!)

These days, however, it isn't just what you buy but where you buy it, and which product line you choose, which matters. Hardly any favourite food needs to be cut out completely as part of a policy of kinder eating when you use the 'Guide to the Kinder Alternatives' on the following pages.

Here, in Part Two, as I am aware that some people can't bear to read the nasty details, I have categorized food for 'kindness' to spare them the necessity. This part provides a complete guide to what to avoid and what to buy, even if you don't (although I hope you will) read the fuller information about every animal given in the A to Z. I start with those products which are still largely supplied by the cruellest of factory-farming systems, indicating the kinder alternatives, and work upwards to those which can be eaten with a free conscience, having escaped the so-called 'progress' of post-war farming.

The kinder alternatives I recommend are all from major supermarkets and stores, or, failing that, from nationwide delivery services. I mean no disrespect to local organic or free-range producers or 'real-meat' butchers whose animals are often even better kept, and on a more desirable small scale. The Soil Association (see pages 126–7) can provide a list of many such producers. But in this book the accent is on accessibility; the aim is that the major supermarkets and stores, who now sell the majority of our animal products and increase their market share each week, should eventually cease to buy ANY of their products from the present cruel factory-farming systems and thus bring such systems to an end.

This is not an impossible struggle. Supporters of intensive farming are already (I am happy to say) beleaguered by environmentalists, country-lovers and those worried by emerging health threats such as salmonella, listeria and BSE. Even the formerly reactionary National Farmers Union has been seen to concede a little ground in recent months. But, in my view, this Agincourt will eventually be won or lost in the aisles of Tesco, Safeway, Sainsbury's, Waitrose, Asda and Marks & Sparks.

If we won't buy it, they can't sell it! So, trolleys at the ready please. CHARGE . . .

THE CRUELLEST FOODS OF ALL

Foie gras and *pâté de foie gras* 62
Veal 63
Eggs from battery hens 66
Chicken meat (and ready-made chicken dishes) . . 70
Turkey (and turkey-meat products) 73
Pork 76
Bacon 79
Sausages 82
Pork pies 83
Rabbit 84
Quail and quails' eggs 85
Frogs' legs 86

ALSO FACTORY FARMED

Ducks 87
Geese 88
Guinea-fowl 89

HIGHLY QUESTIONABLE

Beef (and beefburgers and beef sausages) 91
Cows' milk products (milk, cheese, butter and
    yoghurt) 95
Lobsters and large crayfish 101

QUESTIONABLE

Farmed venison 103
Sheep's milk products 105
Goats' milk products 106
Lamb 107
Farmed fish (salmon and trout) 109
Tuna 112
Eels 113
Snails 114
Wild boar (meat and *pâté*) 115

FOODS YOU CAN FEEL BETTER ABOUT

Game birds 118
Game meat 120
Small crustacea (prawns, shrimps, scampi,
    small crayfish) 122
Shellfish (mussels, oysters, scallops, cockles) 123
Crab. 124
Caviare 124
Free-living fish 125
Organic and near-organic meats 126

NOTE. Fuller details of organic farming, and of four recommended nationwide delivery services for organic and free-range products (Greenway Organic Farms, Ian Miller's Organic Meat, the Pure Meat Company and the Real Meat Company) will be found on pages 126–8 and 139–41.

6. THE CRUELLEST FOODS OF ALL

MANY of the practices involved in producing the foods in this section are a disgrace to successive post-war governments, both Conservative and Labour, who have supported, encouraged and often initiated them. And with *our* money!

We like to think that we are an animal-loving nation and that British Law does not permit cruelty to animals. This is manifestly untrue and can be scientifically proven to be untrue. When it comes to producing cheap food from animals, our law allows many cruelties. (Presumably in order to keep up our world status among the top scorers for coronary heart attacks!)

Although farming is starting to change for the better, the vast majority of foods featured in this section are still produced from animals reared in dreadful conditions, which are described in Part Three of this book. So it is particularly important to choose only the kinder alternatives recommended.

Some of the new, better systems are still far from perfect. But it is important, I believe, to encourage every movement in the right direction if we are to bring a complete end to an appalling era of cruelty.

In this section you will find foie gras and pâté de

foie gras, veal, eggs from battery hens, chicken, turkey, pork, bacon, sausages, rabbit, quail and quails' eggs, and frogs' legs.

FOIE GRAS and PÂTÉ DE FOIE GRAS

Fortunately the cruellest food of all is a product which – at a cost of up to £65 a pound – is eminently resistible by most of us. Even the British government draws the line and forbids its production here. But *foie gras*, which is made from the swollen livers of force-fed geese and ducks, and *pâté de foie gras*, in which the liver is blended with other ingredients, is imported and sold in British delicatessen and stores such as Harrods and Fortnum and Mason.

Those who dine in expensive restaurants are the most likely to be tempted to support this repugnant business. When used as an ingredient in some costly dish, it can be ordered almost unthinkingly. Be firm. Decide in advance to avoid any dishes described on the menu as including *foie gras* or *pâté de foie gras*. A glance at the full description of how it is produced, on pages 170–72, should be more than enough to put you off it for life.

Kinder Pâtés

Pâté de foie should not be confused with *pâté de foie gras*. The former is not produced by force-feeding, and simply means liver *pâté*, usually from chicken or duck. For those who have mislaid their French, *gras* means fat or fatty. That word, plus the high price, is what reveals a content of liver from force-fed geese or ducks.

Clearly, *pâté de foie* is a kinder alternative to *pâté de foie gras*. Indeed, although many *pâtés* contain ingredients from cruelly farmed animals such as pigs, the *foie gras* system is so extreme that any other *pâté* could be said to be a kinder alternative.

VEAL

Kind people don't eat veal, and haven't done so for many years since welfare organizations, most notably Compassion in World Farming, drew attention to the horrors involved in the now notorious veal-crate system. As the much-publicized cruelty involved was putting people off the product, our veal industry had no vested interest in defending it, and in January 1990 the veal crate was banned by law in Britain. A clear example of the power of caring consumers.

Does this mean that you can now eat veal, any veal, with a clear conscience? Sadly, not. Most veal eaten in Britain is imported from Holland where the crate system still predominates. Our government also allows British dairy calves to be exported to Holland and reared in the very system that it has outlawed here. EEC regulations, making some modest improvements to the brutal life of the poor little European veal calf, are in the pipeline. But they won't come into effect for several years. Even then, this won't be a meat that any animal-lover will be able to feel happy about eating.

Most veal served in British restaurants comes from the Dutch crate system. Chefs, particularly those from France and Italy, still tend to insist on meat of near-white colour, which can only be produced by depriving sickly calves of the iron they crave.

Veal from kinder systems is pink, sometimes quite a deep shade, but colour is not a totally reliable indication of a kinder system. Dutch producers tend to export the crate-produced veal, which has become pink by accidental means (urine licking), to Britain, as other Europeans are more insistent on whiteness.

Please don't eat veal in restaurants. If you know a veal-serving restaurateur, try to coax him to buy British veal. And if you buy veal yourself, choose it from the kinder sources below.

Kinder Alternatives

Today, more humanely produced veal is easily obtainable. Some supermarkets insist on an 'only British' policy. Others still import from Holland, but of these some have taken at least one step forward in terms of animal welfare by insisting on the 'group-housing' system used by one major Dutch producer. If you buy veal, it is particularly important to be very choosy about where you buy it.

THE KINDEST VEAL

There is no such thing as 'organic veal', but **The Pure Meat Company**,* *which follows high animal-welfare Conservation Grade standards, can deliver what is probably the most kindly produced veal available. Theirs is what is known in the trade as 'grey veal'. The colour is different, but the meat is still very tender, much healthier and better tasting, and no creature has suffered a life of misery in order to produce it. Pure Meat Company calves suckle and graze with their mothers in the field, as do the best-kept*

* Addresses of firms offering home delivery services, if not given in the text, are on pages 139–41.

beef calves. The only real difference is that they are slaughtered earlier – at about eight months. The company supplies veal cutlets, joints, escalopes and lean minced veal.

KINDEST SUPERMARKETS FOR VEAL

Undoubtedly **Safeway** *and* **Sainsbury**'s*, who insist on an 'only British' policy, are the kindest stores for veal. British veal calves don't enjoy the freedom to graze in the fields, but, indoors, they are more humanely reared, in terms of space and comfort, than those in other European countries. Most are reared in barns, on farms, in groups of about thirty. Conditions will vary from farm to farm, but for most of their lives they have space to move around and are provided with some straw or other fibrous matter for bedding and to satisfy their need to ruminate. Being unnaturally fed on milk, they expel large quantities of near-liquid excrement, which makes it hard to keep them comfortable. But certainly the British veal system is much kinder to animals than that practised in other European countries.*

OTHER SUPERMARKET VEAL

Marks & Spencer *and* **Tesco** *sell Dutch veal, but both these stores at least guarantee that it comes from the 'group-housing' system. (**Waitrose** also import their veal from the Netherlands, but cannot guarantee that it is all from the 'group-housing' system.*

'Group-housed' Dutch veal calves have the companionship of others of their kind (very important for herd animals), and some iron and a little straw on which to ruminate, but no bedding. They live and lie on hard slats and have very little room for movement. This system, which has been encouraged by British retailers, is, in welfare terms, an improvement on the crate but still is hardly a kind way in which to keep living creatures.

EGGS FROM BATTERY HENS

No food is more universally condemned and more universally consumed than the ubiquitous battery egg. The vast majority of Britain's eggs are still produced in this system and many, in various guises, slip down the throats of even well-meaning consumers. Vegetarians, too caring to eat meat, sometimes order, instead, dishes containing eggs of unknown origin – almost certain to be 'battery'. Arguably, in terms of cruelty to animals, they would be better off tucking into a lamb chop.

Of course, you never actually see a battery egg which reveals itself as such. The Ministry of Agriculture, ever supportive of vested interests in the factory-farming industry, refuses the welfarists' not unreasonable request that battery eggs should be labelled as such. This lack of labelling encourages our desire to delude ourselves as we buy 'farm-fresh brown eggs', or battery eggs sold under some other equally misleading description.

We all know that the battery system involves cramming hens into almost unbelievably small cages. They are packed in so tightly that the five hens in such a cage do not even have room to stand up together – one or more must squat. The cage roof is so low that the hen must stand with her head permanently bowed, her feet are on harsh wire. We do not allow her even the air above her head, nor the ground beneath her feet.

Longevity is no bonus for the factory-farmed creature – the egg-layer has to endure such conditions for more than a year.

Kinder Alternatives

Clearly, the caring shopper should look for the words 'free range'. Read my lips: F-R-E-E R-A-N-G-E, not 'farm fresh' or any other deliberately misleading description. Even if they were 'laid today', they were laid in a cage.

There are, however, some worrying aspects involved in today's free-range egg production. Some of the worse large-scale producers are cramming overlarge flocks of many thousands of 'free-range' layers into big buildings ill-designed for easy exit.

The solution to this problem is certainly NOT to buy battery eggs and thus send a 'don't care' signal to the supermarkets. One of the factors which has most convinced them of increased consumer concern about the welfare of farm animals is the major increase, in recent years, of sales of free-range eggs. This has triggered off many free-range systems in other areas of animal rearing. So, by buying free-range eggs you are making a tactical vote for kindness and posting it direct to the powerful people who can do most to bring about change. Since supermarkets are already commendably competing to show that 'Our table birds are *freer* range than yours!', I suspect that it won't be long before the same attitude is applied to eggs as well.

Here are the alternatives available at present:

FREE RANGE
All eggs labelled as such

BARN EGGS
The 'barn' system is better for the hen than the present battery system. ANYTHING is. It would take genius to develop anything worse. The hens in this system, at present, are kept indoors but are not caged. They are provided with wooden bars on which to perch and – particularly important for the hens' welfare – nest-boxes in which to retire to lay their eggs. However, legislation about stocking density allows dreadful over-crowding – and, in turn, this often leads to aggression and injury.

The barn system is best thought of as 'a step in the right direction', away from the battery cage, but leaves much to be desired in its present form. There are hopeful signs of further improvements to it – if consumers keep demonstrating that they are willing to pay a little more for the products of kinder systems.

RSPCA-APPROVED EGGS
Concerned about the large degree of animal suffering involved in the present systems of egg production, the RSPCA has now formulated a list of welfare guidelines for egg-laying hens. These are based on the needs of the bird to lay her eggs in a nest, to roost on a perch, to scratch and dust-bathe and to have adequate space to move and behave

freely. They combine welfare concern with scientific knowledge and practical experience. Producers who adhere to these standards will be able to put a special welfare label on their eggs – and the RSPCA hopes that they will be in the shops some time in 1991. Look out for them!

SMALL-FLOCK FREE-RANGE EGGS

Remarkably, despite the disproportionate difficulties imposed on them by recent legislation, some small local free-range egg producers still exist. This provides you with an opportunity to buy from source – often a farm shop – and to see for yourself that the hens have plenty of space and do not display the signs of injury and feather-pecking (semi-bare backs) which indicate that all is not well with the conditions in which they are kept.

Eggs from small free-range flocks are often on sale in small local shops, fishmongers, delicatessens, etc. So too, however, are battery eggs. Do not assume that eggs labelled 'locally laid' or 'healthily fed' are free-range unless the label actually uses the word 'free-range'. Some shops now display pictures of their free-range flocks and the conditions in which they live, as well as the label. An excellent reflection of our commendable new desire to know how our farm creatures are kept.

KIND QUICHE!

*In a number of their stores, **Marks & Spencer** now sell a quiche lorraine made from free-range eggs. Certainly the first of many more convenience meals using animal products from the kinder systems, if customers prove willing to pay the small extra cost.*

CHICKEN MEAT (and ready-made chicken dishes)

'Cram them in so tight that, if you take one out, they all fall over – that's the way to make money!' This helpful piece of advice, passed on by an experienced chicken-meat producer, nicely sums up the broiler business – a massive industry which has taken intensive farming to the ultimate, bred one of the fastest-growing creatures on earth (out of the egg and into the curry in just seven weeks!) and discovered how to cram as many as a hundred thousand of them into one windowless building.

The broiler chicken endures a wretched little life and fittingly rewards us with near-tasteless meat which is curried, marinated, garlicked, sauced and spiced to supply, by the million, those chilled, frozen and tinned convenience meals.

Kinder Alternatives

No problem, these days, in finding a better-kept chicken. Boredom with the tastelessness of factory-farmed birds and health and cruelty concerns have greatly increased the demand for free-range birds. Nearly all supermarkets stock them, both whole and portion packed. In some areas you can still find small local producers who keep chickens as they like to live – in small flocks. But see for yourself before you buy. There are also 'little local broiler houses'! Organically reared chickens are rather thin on the ground but *Greenway Organic Farms* can deliver French organic chicken.

KINDEST SUPERMARKET CHICKENS
Tesco *sells the most kindly farmed of the supermarket free-range chickens, having acquired exclusive rights to a special breed of French bird which is allowed to roam freely. All their free-range chickens are reared*

in a huge forest area in south-west France, which extends for a hundred square miles. Here, some six hundred French farmers have got together in a scheme which combines more humane poultry farming with the bulk-marketing demands of the supermarkets.

These chickens are not fenced in. They are kept in chicken-houses (only five hundred birds in each, which is very few by today's standards) for the first two or three weeks of their lives, and when they are later released they automatically return to roost at night. Bushes and trees provide the security cover which encourages them to roam and forage. They find 10 per cent of their own natural feed and the rest is corn, which is given to them.

The birds are a local breed, native to the forest, and slower-growing than the broiler, which allows them a longer, thirteen-week, life. They have much more flavour and are available in portion packs as well as whole.

OTHER KIND SUPERMARKET CHICKENS

Marks & Spencer, *and most supermarkets, buy their free-range chickens from a specialist company in Northern Ireland called Moy Park. This company has devised a system of keeping chickens in today's usual large numbers, but in a manner which is certainly a big improvement on the dark broiler-house prison.*

Moy use small producers to rear their birds. Each practises the same system. The chickens are of the same breed as those destined for the broiler-houses and are initially reared in the same way by Moy, but at three and a half weeks, when they no longer need heat (and before conditions start to get really dirty and cramped indoors), they are moved into the free-range buildings on the small farms.

Oddly enough, the main problem with 'free-range' chickens lies in coaxing them out to range freely. Chickens are nervous birds and their natural habitat would consist of trees and bushes, not open fields. Their main fear is attack from above — the hawk is their natural predator. The Moy buildings are well designed, long and thin and with doors opening all along, to encourage easy exit. Now the company is planting the grassland area with trees and shrubs and installing 'protective' rows of fencing which encourage the birds to spend more of their day outdoors.

A typical Moy free-range hen-house would accommodate many hundreds of birds. However, pecking problems, which increase with maturity and often afflict over-large egg-laying flocks, tend not to be a problem in the production of these younger table birds, killed at eight to nine weeks.

The extra price you pay for 'free-range' is justified in the better life of the bird and the better texture of the flesh compared with that of the almost immobile broiler-house bird.

All **Iceland** frozen-food stores now sell Moy Park free-range chickens.

Asda now sell a new range called 'Farmhouse Chickens'. The system which produces them, while not as good as free-range, is a step forward, in welfare, from the conventional broiler-house. These 'Farmhouse' birds live in broiler-houses which have been converted to allow daylight, fresh air and good ventilation. This is an important improvement, as anyone who has stood inside an unconverted broiler-house will be aware; the ammonia rising from *birds' faeces makes human eyes stream. It appears to be just as painful for the birds, and producers have admitted that many go blind. The 'Farmhouse' bird, or 'Premium' as it is sometimes called, is spared this suffering and also given a little more space. The drier litter in these ventilated buildings also cuts down incidence of hock burn, suffered by so many broiler birds.*

TURKEY (*and ready-made turkey dishes*)

The turkey sold in most supermarkets and shops is factory-farmed in dark secrecy, behind closed doors, mainly by a small number of large producers. All factory farmers are anxious to conceal their rearing methods from public and press, but the turkey industry is obsessive in this respect. Clearly, it has much to hide.

I first approached the British Turkey Federation in the winter of 1989, to ask if I could take a look at the factory of any one of the two hundred turkey producers they represent, accounting for 95 per cent of UK-produced turkey. All too busy, in the pre-Christmas rush, it seemed. I tried again throughout the following summer, and was unsurprised by further excuses.

In fact, much of what goes on in this business is well documented. Many turkeys are reared in a similar way to broiler chickens, crowded into purpose-built sheds in large numbers. Although each bird is allocated a little more space, turkeys are unable to live in such unnatural and stressful conditions without aggression and tend to peck at each other relentlessly. This, and the fact that they have been bred to put on weight at a greater rate than their legs can comfortably support, results in much suffering. The cruel process often involved in the slaughter of the turkey has been described as 'diabolical' by a veterinary expert. Please buy turkey only from the following kinder sources:

Kinder Alternatives

These days there are easy ways to find a turkey you can feel better about, since free-range birds are becoming widely available in the major stores.

Often you can find a local producer of free-range turkey. But don't assume that small and local necessarily means free-range – unless you can see for yourself. Some small local producers rear turkeys in dismal sheds in conditions no kinder than those of factory farms.

KINDEST SUPERMARKET TURKEY

From Easter 1991, **Tesco** *will be selling a special breed of free-range turkey from the same forest region in France which supplies their now famous free-range chickens of the Dudley Moore commercials. These are certainly turkeys you can feel better about. Happily, they are going on sale all the year round. They will be the only free-range turkeys sold by Tesco.*

The birds live on pasture land at the edge of the forests and are not fenced in at all. Initially, they are kept in poultry-houses for three weeks, and thereafter they return there automatically each night. These turkeys live considerably longer than intensively reared birds – up to seven months compared to four months or less. They are fed a more natural diet, and grow more slowly to a maximum weight of 11 lb for Christmas and just 5–7 lb throughout the year. This spares them the great pain so often endured by the intensively reared turkeys, which are bred and fed to reach weights which their legs cannot support properly.

OTHER KIND SUPERMARKET TURKEYS

Marks & Spencer *have been encouraging English and*

Irish producers to 'liberate' some of their turkeys, and now fresh free-range birds are widely available in M & S stores prior to Christmas. These birds are kept in the warmth in rearing houses for the first five weeks, and then moved on to free-range farms for the remaining seven to eight weeks of their lives. Most of the farms used are small mixed family farms which have suitable existing housing in the form of lambing houses, hay sheds, etc. This is good for the turkeys, and means they are kept in flocks of hundreds rather than huge flocks of thousands. It also illustrates how a return to 'free-range' can benefit the small farmer. Unlike chickens, turkeys are hardy and adventurous birds and need no encouragement to make full use of the areas of grassland provided for them.

Safeway sell frozen free-range turkeys during the Christmas season; **Sainsbury**'s sell fresh and frozen free-range turkeys at Christmas and Easter; **Waitrose** stock the frozen free-range birds all year round.

DELIVERED TO YOUR DOOR

Three welfare-oriented meat producers can deliver free-range Christmas turkeys to your door: **Greenway Organic Farms** *(whose birds are organically reared, of course),* **The Real Meat Company** *and* **The Pure Meat Company**. *It is wise to place Christmas turkey orders before the end of November. If you are looking for a change, the Pure Meat Company have some imaginative and exotic free-range poultry alternatives, which are described in their product list.*

PORK

Pigs, often among the most cruelly abused of all farm animals, are known to be at least as intelligent as dogs. Picture your dog permanently chained to the ground or confined in a metal-barred stall little bigger than her own body. This is still the lifestyle of the majority of breeding sows which give birth to the piglets fattened up for most of the pork, sausages and bacon now sold in Britain.

As I explained in Chapter 2, scientific research suggests that pigs subjected to this treatment, not surprisingly, seem to suffer from psychiatric disorders. Clearly also in need of psychiatric help are those leaders of the National Farmers Union who (appearing to have overlooked such research) actually believe that pigs might not object to living like this: 'Existing scientific knowledge is unclear on the extent to which pigs actually *need* space, or whether close confinement causes distress,' they reassure us, in a leaflet about the pig industry.

Please read the real facts about the pig industry on page 195–202. And please start to release pigs from their chains, as you so easily and quickly can, by buying pork only from the kinder sources described here.

Kinder Alternatives

Better systems are being introduced into the pig industry, and a minority of breeding sows and fattening piglets are now kept in better conditions – free-range, or at least loose-housed and on straw. Many major stores have begun to sell pork from these more kindly kept pigs, and wait to know whether you are prepared to pay a little more for what is also a much superior meat in taste and texture. Or whether you prefer to support extreme cruelty by buying pork of unknown origin.

Tesco, who introduced a kinder range of pork into a few branches last year, showed me their free-range breeding sows, living in fields, each with comfortable accommodation and straw bedding. I was assured that within months thousands more pigs could be kept in similar conditions, if customers proved willing to pay the slightly increased price. Step by step they would be willing to switch all their producers to such systems. *Marks & Spencer* already have. Others will follow if you buy only the pork – now so easily available – from these humane systems.

KINDEST SUPERMARKET PORK

Marks & Spencer *must take the credit for having led the way in humane methods of pork production. Since last autumn, ALL their fresh pork (although not all their sausages and bacon) has been produced on farms where the parent pigs live continuously outdoors. The young pigs are born in these natural conditions. The sows build straw nests, in their individual ark-shaped houses, when they are ready to give birth. Interestingly, producers are finding that the mortality rate of young piglets in this humane system is only half that of the intensive systems where pigs give birth on hard floors in* metal-barred farrowing crates. When they are allowed sufficient exercise to strengthen their legs and the use of a straw nest, sows rarely flop down and crush their young. The piglets are fattened up in straw-filled barns. These provide a considerable improvement in environment on the barren, dimly lit and windowless sheds where many of their kind are kept on hard-slatted or metal-mesh floors with no straw for comfort, bedding or play.

All M & S fresh pork chops, steaks, escalopes and joints are now produced from pigs kept in this more humane system.

At **Tesco**, the pork labelled 'Traditionally Reared Prime Norfolk Pork' is the special range you can feel better about. (Unlike M & S they also sell pork from intensive systems, so look out for the label.) This is available in many of their branches, in a large variety of cuts and joints, and is packed on distinctive blue trays with the red seal that identifies their 'Traditional Range'. Parent pigs live the happier life described above. Piglets have access to outdoor pens for the first half of their lives before being fattened up on straw in barns. **Asda** are introducing a special range of Conservation Grade pork into many of their stores. (The Conservation Grade label is always an excellent guarantee of a high standard of animal welfare, as well as of healthier rearing methods. The system is similar to the organic one, but allows just a little more leeway in the use of preventive medications.)* These breeding sows will be free-range and their offspring reared in humane

---

* See pages 126–8 for an explanation of organic and Conservation Grade meat.

conditions, part outdoors and part indoors on straw.
Waitrose *has a special range of pork from animals reared under less-intensive conditions. This is labelled 'Traditional English Pork' and is available only from their service meat counters. All the sows are outdoors, either in grass paddocks or deep straw yards. The piglets are indoors, but are also provided with plenty of straw. Again, Asda and Waitrose also sell intensively reared pork, so make sure you are buying the right lines.*

    Iceland *stores also sell pork chops, shoulder and leg from pigs reared in kinder systems. The label to look for here is 'Naturally Reared Prime British Pork'.*

    It is so easy to buy more kindly produced pork these days that no genuine animal (or good food) lover would buy anything else.

BACON

Pigs reared to produce bacon are even more likely to be kept in cruel intensive systems than those kept to produce pork. About 60 per cent of the bacon sold in

Britain comes from overseas, mainly Holland and Denmark, where systems are highly intensive. The disposal of pig manure is an even greater problem in these countries than in ours, and the provision of straw or other bedding would add to the bulk. So the pigs live and sleep on concrete or metal slats.

British bacon is mainly produced by a few giant companies who use similar systems. Piglets being fattened up for bacon take a few weeks longer to be ready for slaughter than those reared for pork. Factory farmers are not inclined to add to their costs, in this competitive business, with such frivolities as providing a little comfort for their beasts.

Bacon, I'm afraid, is one of the cruellest foods you can buy, unless you choose only bacon from the sources described below.

Kinder Alternatives

Sadly, such are the economics of the bacon business, kindly produced bacon is not as easy to obtain at present as 'better kept' pork, but I expect this situation to improve during the coming months. Keep checking those supermarket labels. At the time of going to press, only one major store, Marks & Spencer, was selling bacon guaranteed not to come from pigs in highly intensive systems. (The label 'Traditionally Cured' on Sainsbury's bacon refers, of course, only to the method of curing bacon and not to the treatment of the pigs.)

Your rewards for buying only bacon from better-kept animals will include a hugely improved flavour – bacon that tastes like bacon used to taste!

KINDEST SUPERMARKET BACON
Alone among the major food stores at present, **Marks & Spencer** *sell a recently introduced range of bacon*

produced from pigs kept in considerably more humane conditions than other animals reared to produce this product. This is a special range, to date only available in their major stores and labelled 'Free Range'.

This range – Marks & Spencer's also sell bacon from other sources – represents a major step forward in welfare for both breeding sows and their offspring. The sows live free-range, with individual housing and straw bedding which they make into nests when ready to give birth to their young. The piglets which are fattened up for bacon also spend most of their lives out of doors. This is a particularly welcome development. Even in some of the better systems of modern pig farming, fattening piglets are usually reared indoors. The M & S free-range bacon piglets will spend just the last third of their lives group-housed indoors on straw.

This is the only store-bought bacon that can be recommended, at present, to those concerned about the humane treatment of farm animals.

DELIVERED TO YOUR DOOR

The Pure Meat Company *do nationwide home deliveries of Conservation Grade smoked and unsmoked bacon from a system in which both the breeding sows and their piglets are particularly well kept. The sows are free-range. The piglets suckle from their mother for six to eight weeks – more than twice as long as those in intensive systems, where the aim is to stop the milk and re-mate the sow as swiftly as possible. The piglets also have a longer life than intensive bacon pigs and live out of doors until they are about four months old, only spending their final two months indoors loose-housed on straw.*

Ian Miller's Organic Meat *can deliver smoked*

and unsmoked back bacon, collar and streaky bacon. Both breeding sows and bacon piglets live free-range and, again, the piglets will live twice as long with their mothers as those in intensive systems and have a longer and very much happier life.

Piccards Farm Products of Guildford are another excellent source of delicious bacon from pigs and progeny which spend the whole of their lives grazing outdoors on organic land. They only deliver in the region of the A3, but are within striking distance of London. They also produce splendid sausages and hams. Phone 0483 35364 for details.

SAUSAGES

The pork used in British sausages does not, as you might imagine, come from spent breeding sows. Nearly all of this is exported to make German sausages. Ours are made from the trimmings of joints and chops, the head meat and, quite often, mechanically recovered meat (MRM) made from crushing together the bones and otherwise inedible bits and pieces of pig at the slaughterhouse. The meat is mainly from intensively farmed pigs reared for pork rather than bacon. The beef in beef sausages is usually made from a similar range of bits and pieces of the animal, largely head, neck, flank meat and MRM.

Kinder Alternatives

Three major stores, *Marks & Spencer*, *Tesco* and *Waitrose* now sell a special range of sausages guaranteed to be made from the meat of pigs reared in more humane free-range systems. For kinder beef sausages, see page 95.

KINDEST SUPERMARKET SAUSAGES

Marks & Spencer *have recently introduced a special range of sausages, produced from pigs kept in high-*

*welfare systems, to their major stores. They are
labelled 'Free Range'.*

*In fact, the meat comes from the pigs which are
reared to produce their 'kinder bacon' described on
the previous page, so the same standards apply.
These pigs also live a few weeks longer than pigs
whose meat is usually used for sausages. Certainly a
sausage you can feel better about!*

Tesco *now sell a special range labelled 'Traditional
Pork Sausages' in all their larger stores. They are
packaged with the red seal used on their 'Traditional
Range' products, and the meat comes from systems
in which breeding sows are free-range and the piglets
are reared part outdoors, part indoors on straw.
The* **Waitrose** *range of kinder sausage carries the
same label, 'Traditional Pork Sausages'.*

*Take care to check for these special labels in each
case. Not all the sausages sold by these stores are
from these better systems at present, but they could
be soon if you insist on buying only the kinder
products!*

DELIVERED TO YOUR DOOR
The Pure Meat Company *and* **The Real Meat
Company** *each offer a range of unusual gourmet sausages (with fillings such as lamb and mint or pork and
garlic) as well as straightforward pork bangers of highly
superior flavour.*

PORK PIES
During the past few months, many better meat products
have been introduced into the supermarkets – among
them, the first 'kind pork pie'!

KINDEST SUPERMARKET PORK PIE
Tesco's new 'Traditional Pork Pie', now available in
all their major stores, is made from the meat of animals
which have been humanely reared to supply their 'Traditional' range of fresh pork. Both the farming and the
baking hark back to a previous era. The pie is based on
an 1820 recipe.

RABBIT

In the wild, rabbits are highly active creatures and
spend their day in social groups, busily involved in
eating, exploration and play. In captivity, for meat production, they are incarcerated for life in small wire cages.
These mini-factory-farms, in sheds and garages all over
Britain, are no less nasty for being small.

Rabbit keepers have a tendency to go on at great
length (hence, perhaps, the expression 'rabbiting on')
about their devotion to these poor creatures, but, no,
sorry, there is some pressing reason why you can't see
their rabbits right now, next week or next year. I found
many of these people to be a secretive and singularly
unattractive lot.

All rabbit meat sold in supermarkets and nearly all
that sold elsewhere comes either from these sources or
from China. The Chinese meat is usually diced, darker
in colour and sold in frozen packs. There, I am told,
peasants rear rabbits in colonies in pits surrounded by
close bamboo fencing. Whether they live a better life
than the captive British rabbit is hard to say. It could
hardly be worse.

Kinder Alternatives
Only, I'm afraid, the wild rabbits sold by butchers who
sell game. Often these are sold unskinned.

QUAILS and QUAILS' EGGS

The quail business is very much a microcosm of the broiler-chicken and battery-hen business. Much smaller, but with little more to commend it from the point of view of the birds. Quails raised for meat are normally given more space than the unfortunate broiler chickens but, being particularly active, flighty creatures, possibly suffer as much. Those I saw were a sickening sight. And those pretty little speckled eggs usually come from quails kept in a very similar way to the much-abused battery hen.

Kinder Alternatives

Tesco, who sell such an excellent range of free-range poultry from France, can supply your kinder quail for roasting from the same source. I know of no supermarket source of more kindly produced quails' eggs. Some small-holders keep just a few birds in good conditions and sell their eggs locally. But smallness does not guarantee kindness in the quail business. A good producer will be happy to let you see the birds (which won't have bare backs from feather-pecking attacks!).

KINDEST SUPERMARKET QUAIL

Tesco *wins for quail. All those they sell (in about 120 branches at present) are imported from a French producer who rears them in a kinder way than most of those reared in Britain. Because they would fly away, quail can't be kept completely free-range, but this is the next-best thing. The birds live in a large 'aviary', surrounded by netting, which is 5 m (about 16 ft) high. They have grass on the ground, branches and perches, and room to fly around, in addition to indoor accommodation. These are slower-growing birds than the indoor-reared quail, and taste better: they are fed on cereals and soya.*

FROGS' LEGS

Short of a motorway, there is no fast way to kill frogs. They die slowly and horribly in the Third World countries which export them. Then the pests, which would have fed the frogs, consume the crops. So the poor countries import polluting pesticides from the West, which cost them more than they make from exporting the frogs. Which is why India, once a major exporter, has rightly banned this trade.

Only uncaring oafs consume frogs' legs. If you come across them, try making them digest the full details on pages 167–8. And do tell them about the flies, crawling over the frogs' legs often dumped on factory floors. If they don't care about kindness, that might do the trick!

A French label on a can of frogs' legs usually means only that they have been canned there, after being imported from countries like Bangladesh and Indonesia.

Kinder Alternatives

With a little struggle, it is quite possible to survive without frogs' legs.

7. ALSO FACTORY-FARMED

FEW edible creatures have escaped the attentions of the factory farmers in this dark age for animals and birds. Even ducks, geese and guinea-fowl are now factory-farmed, although the systems used to rear them are generally not as extreme as those endured by the creatures featured in the previous section. Only buy them, as they are conventionally reared today, if you think it right to treat living creatures as machines, deprive them of virtually all opportunity to exercise their normal behaviour patterns, keep them crowded together in sterile sheds, and fatten them up as fast as you can for the kill. Otherwise, please choose the kinder alternatives I suggest.

In this section you will find ducks, geese and guinea-fowl.

DUCKS
Ducks generally live in better conditions and suffer less than broiler chickens – but what a dreary life they lead. Nearly all ducks served and sold in Britain are factory-farmed. Kept in their thousands in huge sheds they stand or sit out their existence of just over seven weeks. Watch the ducks in the park, dabbling, splashing, exploring, to

see the kind of life for which ducks were designed – and what these poor little meat machines are missing.

Kinder Alternatives

Wild duck, when you can get it (see page 119), provides an occasional alternative. Free-range ducks aren't as easily available in the supermarkets as free-range chickens; most don't sell them at present. But things are changing fast, and *Tesco* will almost certainly have free-range ducks by sometime in 1991. Keep your eyes open for free-range labels, and meanwhile assume that all supermarket ducks, duck portions and duck dishes, apart from those mentioned below, are from factory-farmed birds. At present, it is best to look out for a local small producer or buy your ducks from the excellent home delivery services specified below.

KINDEST SUPERMARKET DUCKS
In a limited number of their stores, **Marks & Spencer** *sell whole, boned free-range ducks from small farms in France.* **Sainsbury**'s *sell a frozen free-range duck, but only over the Christmas period.*

HOME DELIVERY OF DUCKS
Greenway Organic Farms *can deliver organically reared Barbary ducks from France;* **The Pure Meat Company** *Conservation Grade free-range ducks and* **The Real Meat Company** *free-range ducks can also be delivered.*

GEESE

Goose, unless chosen with care, no longer provides a kind alternative to the often cruelly abused turkey for Christmas dinner. Many of those sold in supermarkets and butchers' shops are now factory-farmed and no longer allowed to pursue their normal, lively behaviour patterns as the 'intelligentsia' of the poultry world.

Kinder Alternatives

Traditionally reared geese are often still obtainable from local farms and, fortunately, they are usually recognizable in the butchers' shops. While the factory-farmed goose will be near-white, the skin of the genuinely free-range bird will be a golden-yellow colour, from the carotene in the grass on which they graze.

KINDEST SUPERMARKET GEESE

Marks & Spencer *sell traditionally reared free-range geese which are imported from small mixed farms in France. These are on sale in about thirty of their larger branches in the week before Christmas. Check at your local M & S to see if supplies are expected.*

*   **Sainsbury**'s *frozen and fresh geese are all free-range and are available over the Christmas period.*

DELIVERED TO YOUR DOOR

Goodman's Geese *of Walsgrove Farm, Great Whitley, nr Worcester, Worcs WR6 6JJ (Tel. 0299 896 272) can deliver a free-range goose for Christmas if you place your order by November at the latest. The delivery charge of approximately £10 can be reduced if you get together with a neighbour and order two.*

The Real Meat Company *and* **The Pure Meat Company** *also deliver free-range geese, but again suggest that you order early, November at the latest. Phone them for cost and delivery charge. For those who plan to feed vast hordes of relatives and friends, the Pure Meat Company can also supply a five-bird roast – a boned, rolled goose, stuffed with a turkey, a chicken, a pheasant and a pigeon, all free-range.*

GUINEA-FOWL

Don't make the mistake of thinking that guinea-fowl live the free life of 'game'. Far from it. In Britain these are factory-farmed birds, kept in sheds for eight weeks and then usually killed in poultry slaughterhouses. As lively, flighty, semi-wild creatures which love to perch high in trees, they are clearly most unsuited to this sterile existence. Most guinea-fowl are reared on one large factory farm in Norfolk. Don't assume that small local producers necessarily provide them with better lives. Some keep them in closer confinement, where they can fare worse.

KINDEST GUINEA-FOWL

Greenway Organic Farms *can deliver organically reared guinea-fowl from France, and it is sometimes possible to discover a small, local, free-range producer.*

8. HIGHLY QUESTIONABLE

ALTHOUGH, with the exception of some beef cattle, the creatures in this section are not factory-farmed, their treatment often involves some highly questionable practices which make it wise to seek the kind alternatives if you care about animals.

In this section you will find beef (including beef-burgers and beef sausages), cows' milk products (milk, cheese, butter and yoghurt), lobsters and large crayfish.

BEEF (and beefburgers and beef sausages)
These days you don't know what you're getting when you are buying beef, and that's the problem. That steak or joint may have come from a well-reared animal which spent its summers suckling from its mother and grazing in the fields. Or from the unfortunate offspring of a dairy cow, taken from its mother at a few days of age, crowded together with its kind on comfortless slats, fed on cheap and often bizarre foods (some of which, in the past, are thought to have given rise to 'mad cow disease') and slaughtered at just over a year, never having seen the sight of green grass – let alone eaten it.

Beef production is relatively small-scale, so most

retailers and restaurants get their supplies – usually through a wholesaler – from many different sources, rearing animals in many different systems. Often, your guess is as good as that of your butcher or restaurateur about the past history of your steak or beefburger. This even applies to most supermarket beef, other than those lines specially listed below.

Kinder Alternatives

Fortunately, beef you can feel better about and surer about is now easy to obtain. Most supermarkets have recently introduced special ranges of traditionally reared, grass-grazed beef. Those who have tried them confirm huge bonuses in texture and flavour.

Beef that is organically reared offers you the greatest peace of mind, in relation to health. Although bovine spongiform encephalopathy (BSE), 'mad cow disease', could occur on those organic farms which have been more recently converted, it is highly unlikely to do so. The bad farming practices thought to have led to this problem have long been shunned by organic farmers. Most organically reared beef cattle come from suckler herds, which means that the calves will have been fed by their mothers and then grazed with them. Others are the offspring of organically reared dairy cows. None will have been subjected to the misery and disease potential of livestock markets and intensive rearing systems.

KINDEST SUPERMARKET BEEF

Better beef from guaranteed more humane and healthier systems is beginning to inch its way into the supermarkets. But make sure you look out for the specially labelled lines. **Safeway** *has led the field with a delicious range of organic beef, which is proving highly popular. Their* *problem, at present, is to obtain sufficient supplies so that they can stock it in more than the present dozen or so south-eastern branches. But keep looking out for it locally. Fellow shoppers at my local Safeway's rate it the best beef they've ever tasted. It is available in more than twenty different joints, steaks and cuts.*

Asda *– again at only a minority of branches at present – are stocking a splendid humane and healthy beef range which comes from the Pure Meat Company. Look out for that name and the Conservation Grade logo on the label. The products include beef-burgers, as well as joints, steaks, mince and stewing beef.*

Tesco *have introduced their 'Traditionally Reared Prime Beef' (look out for a blue tray with a red seal) into about twelve of their stores, and they will sell it in more if you support it. All the animals are grass-grazed and come from suckler herds, which means that the calves grow up with their mother. Winter housing is of a high standard, with straw bedding. Food is natural and artificial herbicides and pesticides are banned on the pastures.*

Sainsbury's *sell a range of beef which is labelled 'Traditional Beef' and, again, is guaranteed to come from animals reared on pasture during the summer, provided with straw bedding in their winter buildings and fed only on grass, vegetables, cereals and silage. They have also introduced organic beef into one or two of their stores.*

Most of the pre-packed beef sold in **Waitrose** *comes from intensive units (the animals are cereal fed). However, the pre-packed beef labelled 'Speciality Beef' and the Scotch beef sold from the service counters is from grass-grazed suckler herds, so make sure you choose only these.*

Iceland sell a specially labelled range of frozen organic beef – joints of topside, 2 lb packs of mince and ¼ lb beefburgers in packs of four.

DELIVERED TO YOUR DOOR
*All the suppliers described on pages 139–41 will deliver kindly and healthily produced beef to your door. In the case of **Ian Miller's Organic Meat** and **Greenway Organic Farms** this will, of course, be produced to top organic health standards. Those whose local Safeway is not yet stocking organic beef and who fear an outbreak of Mad Grandma Disease in the family, could use these alternative sources of the safest beef you can buy.*

Beefburgers
Anything that is chopped, minced, or put into pies and soups not surprisingly causes us anxiety in these days of food scares. Obviously, when good texture is not necessary there is less chance that a healthily and humanely reared animal will be used. Many parents are now banning beefburgers for their children. The alternative tactic would be to buy 'organic' beefburgers. Or, at least, those from animals fed and reared to high health and welfare standards.

KINDEST BEEFBURGERS
*Many **Iceland** stores now sell beefburgers made from organic beef in their frozen organic range.*

***Ian Miller's Organic Meat** include 4 oz beefburgers (35p each) among the products they will deliver all over Britain. As these take up very little space in the freezer, it could be worth stocking up. Those whose local **Asda** stock the special range of Conservation Grade (very similar to organic in most respects)* *beef from the Pure Meat Company, will find that it includes beefburgers.* **The Pure Meat Company** *will also deliver to your home.*

Beef Sausages

As yet, none of the major stores is selling beef sausages guaranteed to contain meat only from more kindly kept animals.

> KINDEST BEEF SAUSAGES
> **Greenway** *and* **Ian Miller** *can deliver sausages made from the meat of organically reared beef cattle. (The major branches of* **Marks & Spencer**, **Tesco** *and* **Waitrose** *are now selling 'kinder' pork sausages; see pages 82–3.)*

COWS' MILK PRODUCTS (milk, cheese, butter and yoghurt)

To live at peace with your dairy products requires that you close your eyes to an essential element in dairying – the fate of the calves which are born each year so that the cows give milk. To my mind this is a cop-out; may I suggest a helpful compromise instead. Consume less dairy food, and choose the kinder products I describe.

Only a small minority of the offspring of dairy cows will remain on their farm of birth to be reared as herd replacements. The most fortunate of the rest will go to the traditional beef farms but a minority will endure the fate of the intensive beef units. Their suffering, however, is nothing compared to that of the 300,000 British dairy calves exported each year to be incarcerated in the notorious Dutch veal-crate system.

The dairy cow herself, bred and fed to produce so much more milk than her pre-war predecessors, worn out in half the time, is the world's most overworked creature,

much subject to painful conditions of the udder, feet and digestive system as a result. Recently, tests were carried out on British farms to boost her already hugely abnormal milk production by a further 20 per cent. This was the purpose of the genetically engineered growth hormone, BST, which the chemical companies have been struggling to foist on to an admittedly reluctant dairy industry.

Kinder Alternatives

Organic dairy products, now sold in supermarkets and health-food shops, offer improvements in the welfare of the cow and her calf. Organic farmers vary, to some degree, in their treatment of the animals. Some are satisfied with considerably less milk from each cow than today's 'conventional' farmer, others with at least a little less. None push their cows to the full limit. Furthermore, because of her more natural diet, the organically kept cow will be less prone to digestive discomfort and will usually have a longer productive life. She is ensured by Soil Association rules of such humane necessities as soft bedding in winter quarters.

It would be nice to be able to say that no calf born on

an organic farm ever ends up in a European veal crate, but this cannot be guaranteed. Such a fate, however, is considerably less likely for these calves. With the demand for organic products increasing, the majority will be reared on, either as dairy replacements or in organic beef units, and very few will be sent to suffer the cruelty of the markets.

KINDEST MILK

Organic milk is beginning to trickle into the supermarkets, albeit in a somewhat sporadic way. Their problem lies in obtaining supplies, but an enthusiastic response from consumers will increase the pressure on farmers to convert to this system. **Marks & Spencer** *stock organic milk, packed in green cartons, in many of their branches and nearly half of* **Sainsbury**'s *stores now sell organic milk under their own label. Supplies can, however, be depleted due to factors such as shortage of grass during a dry summer spell. So if they dry up for a while, keep watching the shelves.*

In the west of England it is worth checking with your milkman. Some are able to deliver organic milk, supplied by **Unigate**, *and with a Soil Association symbol, direct to your door. In this region, which has a number of organic dairy farms,* **Safeway** *also sell it. Elsewhere, if you find difficulty in tracking down supplies, it is well worth checking out local health-food shops, who sometimes stock organic milk and dairy products from local producers.*

Most of us tend to order much more milk than we need, just in case we run out. The best tactic to achieve a pinta-less each day is to keep cartons of long-life milk in the pantry for such a contingency. Like me, you will probably hate to waste a drop of milk, in view of the suffering its production often involves.

Soya milk, available in many supermarkets, is, of course, the vegan alternative. Even if this is not to your taste, you will probably find it perfectly acceptable in such things as cheese sauces and creamed mushrooms.

Coffee-Mate and other whiteners contain some milk protein, and perhaps the best tactic is to learn to like your coffee black. As a slimming expert I can tell you that this is one of those habits which, once acquired, actually becomes a preference. (Unlike those chocolate cravings, which can keep on creeping up on you!)

See also Sheep's Milk Products, pages 105–6, and Goats' Milk Products, pages 106–7.

KINDEST CHEESES

In terms of animal welfare I see little logic in so-called 'vegetarian cheese'. Usually this is simply cheese made from ordinary milk, but without the rennet – a substance which is taken from the stomach of slaughtered calves. This ignores the issue of what happened to the calf born to drink the milk; quite possibly it was sent off to a fate far worse than early death in a Dutch veal crate.

Organic cheeses give a better guarantee of kinder treatment of cow and calf. Two such cheeses, which are now widely available in supermarkets, are Pencarreg – very much like French Brie, but even creamier and nicer in my opinion – and, more recently, Cardigan Full Fat Hard Organic Cheese. The latter is similar to Cheddar, so it supplies the need for a kinder cheese to grate for toasting, sauce-making and cooking in general. Both of these cheeses *are made with vegetarian rennet. All branches of* **Safeway** *now sell Pencarreg and Cardigan (if you can't find it at the local branch, ask the manager, who can obtain it for you).* **Sainsbury**'s *sell Pencarreg in most stores, and* **Asda** *sell both of these cheeses in some of their West Country branches.* **Tesco** *have recently introduced Organic Cheddar and Biobree Organic Brie from France into many of their stores.*

Rachel's Dairy, *which holds the Soil Association symbol, sells organic cottage cheese (rennet free) in many health-food shops throughout London, the Home Counties, Wales, the west midlands and the north-west, where they supply* **Booths** *supermarkets. The producers of this range of dairy products guarantee that none of their calves is ever sent to market, so you can be sure that none ends up in veal crates.*

KINDEST YOGHURT

At first glance, organic yoghurt seems to be easily obtainable at the supermarkets – but read those cartons with care! Most base their claim simply on the organically grown fruit content. They are not made with organic milk. BioBest and Onken Bioghurt from Germany are two such products, a sensible choice for those concerned about chemical crop sprays, but no kinder to cows than any other dairy product.

However, many branches of **Safeway**, **Sainsbury**'s *and* **Waitrose** *sell Busses Farm Yoghurt, which is made with organic milk, and is now available in apricot and raspberry flavours, as well as plain. This is also sold in many health-food shops, as is the* **Rachel's Dairy** *range of organic yoghurts. With other locally produced 'organic yoghurts' in health-food shops, again take care to check that the label does state that the milk, not just the fruit, is organic.*

KINDEST BUTTER

Butter from organic sources is hard to find. A small number of organic farms produce and sell it locally, and it is worth looking out for **Rachel's Dairy** *butter in health-food shops and delicatessen.*

However, butter can easily be replaced in the diet: by the many healthier vegetable oils when you are grilling and frying, by animal-free White Flora and Trex when you are making pastry, and by Safeway Pure Vegetable Margarine when you are baking or spreading. **Safeway** *now also sell their own brand of soya margarine, which is animal-derivative-free. (You will also find a number of animal-free margarines made by companies like Prewetts and Granose in health-food shops.) Most other margarines and low-fat spreads do, in fact, contain some animal products, usually whey or skimmed milk powder. Peanut butter, of course, is another excellent alternative for spreading.*

LOBSTERS (AND LARGE CRAYFISH)

Everyone knows that most lobsters (and crayfish of similar size) are boiled alive, but the question is: How long do they take to die? Certainly not 'just a few seconds', as

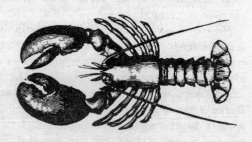

in the case of small crustacea. The lowest informed estimate is twenty seconds – if special care is taken to speed the process – but experiments at Oxford University suggest that they might suffer for two minutes or more. Before that lobsters will have lived for about five years, free in the sea. But count to twenty (to take the most optimistic estimate) and imagine how it feels to be boiled alive for that time. I did, and I don't eat lobster any more.

9. QUESTIONABLE

THE foods featured in this section are not necessarily produced by the cruel methods of modern 'farming'. Some are good – but, like the curate's egg, only in parts. With others there are 'don't-know' areas, as in the case of farmed fish. So I have indicated what pleases me and what worries me, and left you to decide for yourself.

In this section you will find farmed venison, sheep's milk products, goats' milk products, lamb, farmed fish (salmon and trout), tuna, eels, snails and wild boar.

FARMED VENISON

Over the past decade, deer farming has been one of the small fringe areas of British meat production – and smallness has been good for the welfare of the animals. Now this business is expanding briskly, and welfarists are worried that the bad practices of intensive farming will creep in, in the rush to produce more meat more quickly. Already, one agricultural college has been experimenting with a zero-grazing system for deer, keeping them in buildings and yards. Currently, however, deer tend to be among the better-kept farm animals and most are killed with concern to minimize their fear and suffering. They graze in pasture during the summer months, some in wide areas of parkland, others in questionably small paddocks.

Almost alone among farm animals, deer can be dispatched with a quick, clean death – free of trauma, terror and any rough handling. Because they are classed as 'game' in food-production legislation, they can be shot at point-blank range in the field in which they graze. The RSPCA and Compassion in World Farming confirm that this is by far the most humane way of killing these nervous creatures. And any other animal, for that matter. Most of our slaughterhouses leave very much to be desired in their treatment of animals in general. What little inspection there is is largely concerned with hygiene, and the fear and suffering of the animals is generally given a low priority. Now, as the venison business expands, many deer are killed in slaughterhouses. However, a special deer slaughterhouse opened in Hertfordshire recently has been designed with considerably more concern for the welfare of the animals than most.

KINDEST SUPERMARKET VENISON
Sainsbury's is the only supermarket which sells 'field-shot' venison, the slaughter method most preferred by welfare organizations. The animals live in extensive free-range conditions.

DIRECT FARM SALES
More than half the venison sold in this country is still bought direct from deer and farm shops. Send a stamped addressed envelope (at least $8\frac{1}{4} \times 4\frac{1}{2}$ in) to the British Deer Farmers' Association, c/o Mrs Anne Dymond, Holly Lodge, Spencers Lane, Berkswell, Coventry CT7 7BZ, for a list of these farms. Select

those which state that the animals are slaughtered 'on farm'. When visiting, check that the animals graze in reasonably extensive areas, and that, if left in the fields in winter, they have trees, hedging or walls to provide the necessary shelter.

OTHER SUPERMARKET VENISON
Safeway, **Tesco**, **Waitrose**, **Asda** *and* **Summerfields** *all sell farmed venison which has been killed at the special deer slaughterhouse in Hertfordshire to which I have referred. Although this is generally kinder than sending deer to general slaughterhouses, animal-welfare organizations still consider the small-farm method of shooting at point-blank range the most humane.*

SHEEP'S MILK PRODUCTS
Sheep's milk and dairy products are now widely available. Kinder than cows' milk? Probably so, if you take all aspects into account, particularly the disposal of the lambs. Unlike many of the offspring of dairy cows they will not end up in European veal crates, but neither will they grow up with their mothers in green fields. Offspring of dairy sheep are usually reared indoors, on concentrates, for fast conversion into meat.

Sheep dairying, however, is still relatively small-scale. On the farms I saw, lambs were living in small groups, on straw, in traditional airy farm buildings. Certainly a better life than that of most factory-farmed animals. Their mothers, the milking ewes, also seem to fare reasonably well by today's farming standards.

Kind Alternative (to Ordinary Cheese)

Organic sheep's milk cheese, produced to high Soil Association animal-welfare standards, provides another kinder alternative to ordinary cows' milk cheese. Such a cheese, Martin Pitt's Wiltshire White Organic Cheese, is now on sale at *Safeway*.

GOATS' MILK PRODUCTS

I once knew a squadron leader's wife who often used to sleep in the barn with her goats – possibly a reflection on the squadron leader! Nice, nutty people like this, and many more ordinary animal-loving smallholders, still keep goats in a comfortably traditional way, and the majority of British goats live in herds of just two to ten animals. There is a long tradition of goat enthusiasts in Britain.

Today, bigger herds are on the increase, and here 200–500 animals are usually kept together in farm buildings. This means a boring life for the goats, which are not allowed to forage in the fields, but they usually have much more space, plenty of straw and better conditions than are experienced by most intensively farmed animals.

Kids are generally killed quickly, on farm, but more worrying is the fate of those – and also their mothers, at the end of their productive days – which are sent off to markets and slaughterhouses to be killed and sold as meat. Goat meat is particularly popular among Muslim communities. So the goat has more chance than most animals of the halal method of slaughter, which usually means that they are not stunned before being bled to death.

Kinder Alternatives

Short of checking with your small local supplier, there is no way of knowing the fate of the animals which supplied your goat yoghurt and cheese. Cartons usually carry the address of the farm of origin, and caring goat-keepers will appreciate your concern if you inquire. Many, particularly the small ones, go to a good deal of trouble to check out local abattoirs and take the animals along themselves. Those who send their live animals to markets, and an unknown fate, are the ones to avoid. Usually, but not always, this will be the larger-scale goat farmers, who seek some financial return for their meat.

LAMB

You can feel better about the life of the lamb than that of many other widely farmed animals. But not about its death. What a pity that this area of agriculture mars its image with scandals like live exports and frequent lack of concern (other than financial) about the fate of the animals once they leave the farm gate.

Sheep are what is known as 'good grazers'. They neatly nibble their nourishment from short grass on land not fertile enough to grow anything else. By this happy chance of nature they have proved economically resistant to the 'progress' of post-war agriculture. It costs less to keep them outdoors.

Some lambs are reared indoors, usually on straw, but this area of production is small, just about 7 per cent of the whole – and seasonal. These lambs, some from dairy sheep, are kept indoors and fed on concentrates, mainly with the aim of getting 'new season's lamb' into the shops before the naturally reared lambs come on sale at lower prices at the end of May.

Most lambs are slaughtered at about sixteen weeks. It would be comforting if they could end their short lives peacefully but, in fact, nearly 70 per cent are subject to the stress of auction markets. Farmers have gained a modest advantage in EEC subsidies by this method of marketing, and traditionally it is a day out for the farmer. It certainly isn't much of a day out for the sheep! Even meat processors complain that lambs sold via auctions have twice the bruising of those sent direct to slaughter. Still worse is the fate of the half million British sheep and lambs which each year are shamefully allowed to suffer long and harrowing journeys to European slaughterhouses.

Kinder Alternatives

Organic standards usually ensure a much more natural and thus happier life for farm animals than today's more widely practised rearing methods. With ewes and lambs, largely kept outdoors anyway, the difference is not so great. However, both traditional organic practice and economic factors (now that organically reared lamb is in demand from the supermarkets) make it extremely unlikely that organic lambs will be sold by auction or for live export.

Apart from this, the main difference lies in the use of drugs, chemicals and vaccines. Organic sheep are not routinely dosed and vaccinated against common sheep ailments in the same way as their non-organic sisters. Conventional farmers can fairly claim that such treatments protect their animals from suffering. Indeed, humans are vaccinated on a similar basis. Organic farmers counter that their methods of better husbandry, less intensive stocking and rotation of land make such treatments largely unnecessary, and of course drugs can be used on organic farms too if signs of illness or suffering occur.

SUPERMARKET ORGANIC LAMB

Safeway *have introduced organically farmed lamb into about twenty of their stores. This costs, on average, just 15 per cent more than conventionally reared lamb and carries the Soil Association seal of approval. This guarantees, for instance, that the grass grazed by the sheep has not been treated with artificial fertilizers or chemicals for at least two years. Supplies are still limited and it will probably be some time before sales can be extended to further stores.*

HOME DELIVERIES

All the home-delivery services described on pages 139–41 can deliver lamb to your door – and these animals will have been killed without the stress of auction and long transportation. The lamb supplied by **Ian Miller's Organic Meat** *and* **Greenway Organic Farms** *will, of course, have been fed and reared organically.*

FARMED FISH (salmon and trout)

Questionable? Highly questionable? Even cruel? Frankly, I found it hard to determine how to categorize farmed salmon and trout. Certainly there are strong environmental arguments against fish farming but our main concern here is cruelty.

Farmed fish are kept together in vast numbers in small areas of water and their powerful natural instincts are suppressed. They are known to have complex nervous systems and brains, and to be capable of experiencing pain and stress. And yet, peering into a long concrete

tank, containing sixty thousand young trout, I didn't feel the shock and distress of witnessing chained pigs, broiler chickens or battery hens.

Crowded though they are, the fish can swim and don't suffer the complete immobility and often chronic pain endured by so many factory-farmed creatures. Like citizens of the streets of Calcutta, or rush-hour travellers on the London Underground, theirs is not an enviable lot. But it beats being kept in solitary confinement for life in a cell little bigger than one's own body – a commonplace way of treating farm animals today.

Fish, let's face it, are harder to understand than land animals. 'Unease' was how an RSPCA veterinary expert described his organization's attitude to fish farming. It seems as good a summing up as any, in our present state of knowledge.

Salmon, Fresh, Smoked and Canned

More than 90 per cent of the fresh and smoked salmon sold in Britain is farmed salmon. Oddly enough, the only wild salmon most of us eat is the stuff that comes in the cans. This is Pacific-caught salmon, still so profuse that the canners can buy it more cheaply than farmed salmon. If the Japanese continue to empty the Pacific of all forms of life and farmed salmon continues to get cheaper, this situation could well change. Meanwhile, you may boast that your establishment serves only wild salmon, as you pop into the kitchen for the can of John West.

Salmon farming takes place in coastal areas, mainly in Scotland. The young fish are reared in tanks in land-based hatcheries, and then taken (in lorries, boats, even helicopters) to tidal lochs and estuaries where they will live in large cages suspended under the water. They are fed on pellets consisting largely of fish meal and containing a chemical colouring agent to make their flesh pink. Most will be killed around three years after hatching.

Salmon farming gives rise to an associated cruelty. Seals and other wild predators, attracted to such concentrated sources of food, are shot in large numbers by fish farmers.

KINDEST SALMON
Wild salmon is becoming increasingly available in the supermarkets. **Sainsbury's**, **Tesco** and **Waitrose** *sell fresh wild salmon, labelled as such, in some of their branches.* **Safeway** *sells the Irish Seaspray brand of wild Atlantic smoked salmon.*

Trout
Trout farms are very diverse in character. You might find a small local one which keeps fish in earth-bottomed ponds, a large one which uses long rectangular concrete-lined 'raceways', or even one in a Scottish freshwater loch in which trout are kept in underwater cages.

In contrast to so many other areas of modern 'farming' (the darkly secretive turkey industry, for instance) the trout industry practises Glasnost – always a good sign. Send a stamped addressed envelope to the British Trout Association, PO Box 2, Clitheroe BB7 3ED, for a list of trout farms all over Britain, many of which can be visited. Do not revisit those which allow punters to fish

in their highly stocked ponds and return the fish to the water, perhaps several times. A cruel practice!

Usually, trout farmers buy eggs from hatcheries and the tiny, newly hatched fish are kept indoors at first, swimming around in large tanks. Then they are moved into outdoor areas of water. Most trout are killed at about a year after hatching.

KINDEST TROUT

Some branches of **Waitrose** *sell wild salmon trout, and sea trout are occasionally available at fishmongers. Don't assume, however, that even a harbour-side fishmonger is necessarily selling wild salmon or sea trout unless you check. Often they buy them from the farms like almost everyone else.*

TUNA

Conservation and environmental groups are troubled about tuna. Not because these fish don't live a free life in the sea, but because a vast, needless slaughter of dolphins and other sea creatures is very much associated with tuna fishing.

Those huge twenty-five-mile long 'wall-of-death' fishing nets left floating in the Pacific are mainly there to capture tuna. Not skipjack tuna, the kind we mainly eat in Britain, but a much more expensive species called albacore. However, many skipjack are caught in the same nets; some of these are taken to Thailand canneries from which much tuna is exported to Britain.

Kinder Alternatives

The Whale and Dolphin Conservation Society has been negotiating with UK tuna importers and retailers and a 'dolphin-friendly' standard has been agreed. When you see a can of tuna carrying a special WDCS kitemark and 'dolphin-friendly' logo it means that the producers have agreed not to use any tuna caught in drift-nets or by other methods which kill dolphin. They have also agreed to independent, unannounced inspections – as well as to carrying out their own programme of monitoring and inspection. The standards will apply to tuna used in petfood as well as human food.

> ### KINDEST TUNA
> *Although all kitemarks may not yet have appeared on the labels, these are the companies who have signed the dolphin-friendly agreement with the Whale and Dolphin Conservation Society at the time of going to press: Asda, CKS Products, Co-op, David Coutts, A. Donatantonio & Sons, Gerber, Glenryck, Haig Castle, John West, K. J. Lovering, MCM (UK), Premier Foods, Princes, R & A Seafood, Safeway, Saupiquet, Town and Country Petfoods.*

EELS

Eels swim here all the way from the Sargasso Sea and enjoy a particularly long life of seven years or more, in sea and river, before they are caught. Sadly, they are particularly difficult to kill and often endure a rather slow death in salt – which is why I leave you to make up your mind about whether you feel comfortable about eating them.

SNAILS

Were those snails you are offered on the menu born free in far-off Turkey or Greece, or factory-farmed on a polypropylene tray in Britain? Or maybe they grazed on oilseed rape or clover on a free-range farm. It's hard to tell. And how were they killed? Quickly, in seconds, by being dropped, a few at a time, into boiling water? Or slowly, by being immersed in brine for twenty-four hours or more, with the lid of the container weighed down to stop them climbing out. Yuk!

In restaurants it is all very complicated and hard to know just what happened to your snail before you met. Couldn't you order the avocado or a slice of melon instead?

WILD BOAR (*meat and pâté*)

It is easy to assume that wild boar have lived the life of Riley, snuffling around in happy herds in forest glades. Not so, for many years, in this country. Wild-boar keeping is a new farming diversification. Some are allowed to root around in areas of fenced-off woodland, but many are reared indoors. Unfortunately, their legal classification as 'dangerous wild animals' detracts from their lifestyle. The costly fencing required by law results in a tendency to keep them indoors (albeit in straw-bedded pens) or to confine them in small outdoor pens. It also means they must be sent to the slaughterhouse, more traumatic for the animal than being shot on home territory, like game.

THE HEALTHIEST DIET KNOWN TO SCIENCE

Pictured on the following pages is a one-day Western-style menu which comes as close as you can get to health perfection. It is based on new World Health Organization dietary guidelines initiated by one of Britain's most distinguished nutritional experts, Professor Philip James, and gives a clear idea of how much 'animal' food you can healthily afford to eat.

THE KIND FOOD GUIDE

THE menu illustrated represents all that is currently known by science about the type of eating pattern likely to lead to a long and healthy life. No doubt more remains to be discovered in the future. But meanwhile, here is the way in which you should be eating and drinking now if your aim is to be doing handstands at a hundred.

This representative one-day menu for an adult includes foods selected from all those groups now thought to protect us against degenerative Western illnesses such as heart disease and cancers.

Notably excluded is the large quantity of saturated animal fat believed to be the most health-threatening factor in today's typical British menu. Remember that such fat is often not visible to the eye. Even the leanest-looking meat supplies it and it is present in rich quantities in many dairy products.

Even more important than its individual components, however, is the balance of our perfect menu. Today's top nutritionists believe that we should now aim to get between 50 and 70 per cent of our daily calories in the form of cereals and complex carbohydrates (cereals, pasta, rice, potatoes, etc. – the starchy foods). That alone revolutionizes the concept of 'healthy eating'. Having already learned that we can no longer afford three animal-food-based meals, and having therefore abandoned the old 'British cooked breakfast', we must now adjust to the idea that we cannot really afford two such meals, unless we use animal products very sparingly, merely as a garnish! In fact, the pattern of eating which most of us would think of as semi-vegetarian is now supported by mainstream science. Further health 'ingredients' of the perfect diet are described on page vii of this section.

Breakfast. Here we combine two cereals for different health benefits – an ounce of whole-wheat flakes for their dietary fibre, another of cholesterol-lowering oats. The quarter pint of milk is skimmed, of course. For valuable vitamin C there is half a grapefruit, sweetened with a level teaspoon of sugar; a 4 fl oz glass of orange juice would be an alternative. This sugar, and that in the half ounce of raisins, comes within the maximum quantity allowed by the 'perfect diet'.

Lunch: Bean and Pasta Salad with Pitta Bread. This meal provides a variety of valuable protective vegetables – 2 oz red kidney beans, 2 oz diced carrots, 1 oz diced green pepper, 1 oz sweetcorn and a little chopped onion, combined with 1½ oz (dry weight) of pasta. We have used a salad dressing which also adds health benefits: two teaspoons of olive oil, a tablespoon of lemon juice (rich in vitamin C), pepper and a pinch of mustard powder.

Main Meal: Stuffed Herring with Potato, Broccoli and Carrot. A free-living fish, rich in naturally occurring beneficial fats, is combined with broccoli (6 oz) and carrots (4 oz), both outstanding sources of protective nutrients. The potato (6 oz) could be new or baked potato. To stuff the herring we combined still more healthy things – breadcrumbs (1 oz), chopped watercress, the juice and rind of half a lemon and freshly ground pepper. As an additional course there is half an Ogen melon.

Snacks and Drinks: Banana Cinnamon Toast and Fruit.
The average woman's daily requirement of 2,000 calories still
allows a little extra, so we have allowed snacks of the healthy
kind. There is a piece of fruit, and banana cinnamon toast
(made by topping toasted currant bread with a sliced banana
and cinnamon, and grilling for a few moments). Since perfection is the aim, we have avoided now-suspect caffeine (and
alcohol, of course) and chosen the purest natural water.

People talk glibly about a 'balanced diet', not really knowing what it is. The menu pictured is today's scientific concept of a balanced diet: New-Age Eating.

Variety is vital to good nutrition and I am not, of course, suggesting that the same menu should be followed each day. Neither need foods supplying the protective nutrients, or any other important nutrients, be consumed on a daily basis. It is often more realistic to think in terms of several helpings each week. But the perfect menu gives a clear idea of the proportions of cereal, fruit and vegetable, and animal foods that should be eaten.

Calorie requirements vary, but this menu supplies the 2,000 calories most British women can consume daily without gaining weight. Most men could add a further 500, by increasing all quantities by 25 per cent. Other health guidelines incorporated include a maximum limit of six grams of salt and 10 per cent added sugar.

On such a cereal- and vegetable-rich diet there is no need to worry about sufficient dietary fibre – this takes care of itself. And this menu provides MORE than enough protein to satisfy the requirements.

10. FOODS YOU CAN FEEL BETTER ABOUT

THE fish, flesh and fowl featured in this section come from the creatures which live better lives, so generally you can regard them as kinder alternatives to most other animal products. Either they enjoy a largely natural lifestyle (albeit, often, a short one) or they are farmed in a reasonably humane way. Obviously they offer you a safer, healthier choice of animal-based food. Those creatures which live in a natural way have a lower content of saturated fat – which is associated with coronary heart disease and other ailments. They are also less prone to cross-infections and less subjected to dubious medications and feed additives.

Those who don't approve of blood sports may be disappointed to discover that all game birds and animals are featured among these 'foods you can feel better about'. I sympathize with and share their sentiments. But I have to be objective and consider only the life and death experienced by the creature involved. At least the game which ends on the table is almost invariably the product of the shoot, where the basic aim is a quick death. The worse cruelties to hunted animals tend to arise from the chase, which sets out with precisely the opposite intent.

In this section you will find game birds, game meat (wild rabbit, hare, game-shot venison), small crustacea (prawns, shrimps, scampi, small crayfish), crab, caviare, free-living fish and organic and near-organic meats.

GAME BIRDS

These days only a minority of the game birds that end up in shops, supermarkets and restaurants are actually born free. Game shooting is big business. So much so that nature can no longer meet the demand and game farms, using artificial (and sometimes dubious) rearing methods, have taken over. Most game birds are hatched and reared for their first six weeks on these farms. But at least, after that, they are released into a natural habitat and will enjoy reasonable freedom for most of their short lives.

The most fortunate of the game birds will be killed instantly with one shot. Many will be injured and take longer to die. But, in comparison with most poultry in today's factory farms, the game bird lives a life of bliss.

Whether or not you eat game birds, the chances are that they would be shot anyway. This may be a comfort!

Profit comes mainly from the clients willing to pay large sums for the pleasure of a day's shooting – and allowed to keep only a couple of birds. The money which the commercial estates make from selling off the day's bag represents only a small proportion of their income. It is estimated that those operating pheasant shoots make about £20 per bird from the sportsmen compared with little more than £1 from the game dealer.

For the same economic reason, game birds have thus far been spared life imprisonment in factory farms. Because so many game birds are sold off cheap from the shoots, those who have tried to raise them entirely for food have found that they couldn't compete profitably. So you can be reasonably sure that the birds listed below enjoyed some freedom.

Sainsbury's, *Safeway*, *Waitrose*, *Tesco* and *Asda* all sell game, when in season, at their larger branches.

Below I list, first, the birds which are born free, then those which are usually reared in game farms before being released to enjoy some freedom.

BORN-FREE GAME BIRDS

Grouse: *available mid-August to November or December.*

Pigeon: *available mid-September to early May. Some* **Waitrose** *stores sell frozen pigeon throughout the year.*

Woodcock: *not widely available. Sold from mid-November to the end of January in a few branches of* **Sainsbury**'s *and 'high-class' butchers, like* **Harrods** *meat department.*

ARTIFICIALLY REARED GAME BIRDS

Pheasant: *widely available from early November to the end of January and becoming almost as cheap as chicken* *during the season.* **Waitrose** *sell frozen pheasant throughout the year.*

Partridge: *available early September to the end of January.*

Wild Duck (Mallard): *sold in some branches of* **Safeway,** *as well as 'high-class' butchers, from mid-November to the end of January.*

GAME MEAT

The creature which has entirely escaped the attentions of the factory farmer, and lived its life in the wild, clearly offers a kinder and healthier alternative meat. This will be low in saturated fat, free of added hormones, antibiotics, etc., but not necessarily of the residues of the pesticides which drench our countryside.

Demand for game is increasing. Generally, the problem lies in tracking it down in the shops and differentiating between wild and farmed. Here is how to recognize the real thing.

Wild Rabbit

Nearly all the rabbit meat you see in supermarkets and shops is from farmed rabbits. Most of it is produced by intensive methods in an industry which, though small-scale, incorporates all the cruelties of factory farming. The only way to find a rabbit which has lived a happy life is to go to the type of butcher who specializes in game. You find him, usually, in the pricier parts of cities or country towns. Wild rabbits are often hung in the window in full fur. The meat is very different from the farmed rabbit meat – much darker in colour. You can, if you wish, console yourself with the thought that farmers have traditionally regarded rabbits as a pest and countrymen have hunted them for centuries. So this rabbit didn't die entirely for your pie.

Hare

Not widely available, but some branches of **Sainsbury**'s stock portion-packed hare in their chilled meat department during the season from the end of September to the end of February.

Happily no one has yet found a way to cram this glorious free-running creature into a cage. (But don't put it past them!) Hare meat is usually a product of the spring shoots on sporting estates. Here, as the leisure business booms, it is regarded as a valuable sporting quarry, and concern is being expressed about the depletion of the hare population. However, you can reassure yourself that the hare which reaches the shops via the game dealer is not likely to be a product of the cruel sport of hare coursing, as the poor creature torn to bits by dogs is unlikely to remain in an edible state.

Game-shot Venison

Despite the recent growth of deer farming, much of the venison served or sold in Britain, particularly north of the border, comes from wild deer shot as sport or as part of a cull. On the whole, deer shooting is well supervised. Most animals will be killed quickly and cleanly. The poor creatures cruelly pursued to their deaths by appalling people with packs of hounds are unlikely to come into the commerical food chain. Without culling, herds of wild deer would expand beyond the capacity of the land to support them. Many animals would die a lingering death from starvation during the winter months.

Ian Miller's home delivery service can supply game-shot venison.

SMALL CRUSTACEA (*prawns, shrimps, scampi, small crayfish*)

Can you be cruel to crustacea? Some years ago the Scottish Society for the Prevention of Cruelty to Animals tested that question in the courts. They brought a case for cruelty against a woman who dropped live shrimps on to a hotplate for the 'fun' of seeing them jump. The verdict was 'Unproven', largely because few scientists have concerned themselves with the feelings of a shrimp or prawn, and evidence was sparse.

What is known is that crustacea have a nervous system, but nothing that resembles the human brain as closely as does the 'brain' of a fish. As the Scottish shrimps demonstrated, they react to noxious stimuli. Which would suggest that they are subject to pain as a survival mechanism. Let us give them the benefit of the doubt in that respect. At the same time, we might reasonably assume that they don't give too much thought as to whether they are being artificially cultivated (which happens in the case of many prawns and crayfish) or living totally free in the sea. I doubt if they care.

What clearly matters is how humanely they are killed. It is well known that many are boiled alive, like lobsters. The difference lies in the time they take to die, which is very much more quickly. Most experts would say 'in a few seconds'. Their small bodies are quickly overwhelmed by the heat. Other methods employed to kill small crustacea sound equally nasty, but also have the virtue of being speedy. So there are reasonable grounds for feeling better about eating small crustacea than large ones, or than most other species of living creature.

SHELLFISH (mussels, oysters, scallops, cockles)

It is hard to believe the mussel minds too much whether he is sitting around on a rock or hanging around on a rope under a raft, and few of us would rally to the cry of 'Oysters' Rights!', though they too are often semi-artificially cultivated in the sea.

All these creatures have simple nervous systems, but nothing that resembles a brain. They are sensitive to touch, so probably experience pain. Because of their small size they can be assumed to die quickly. If you are making *moules marinières*, you may be comforted to know that the mussel dies in the pan before its shell opens – as soon as its body temperature reaches 30 °C. The shell opening is a mechanical process which occurs after death. Oyster eaters may draw satisfaction from the fact that the vast majority of oysters left in the sea are also eaten alive. One oyster can produce as many as a million offspring in one spawning, out of which only two or three might survive in the highly predatory underwater environment. (But, of course, those oysters don't die with a squirt of lemon in the 'eye'!)

CRAB

There are several consolations for the caring consumer of a fresh crab sandwich. One is that the crab will have enjoyed a reasonably long life in the coastal waters of Britain and will have been caught by an environmentally friendly fishing method. Another is that it won't have been dropped live into boiling water, like the lobster.

Fishing laws dictate that only crabs of four inches or more may be taken from the baited underwater traps in which they are caught and the smaller ones must be released. It takes a crab four to five years to reach the required size.

The crab is killed in a different way from most other crustacea due to its fortunate habit of shedding limbs if boiled alive. To keep it intact it is usually killed before cooking, by being drowned in fresh water, which takes three to five hours.

Could this slow death be even worse? Experts suspect that, as its body fluids are gradually diluted it just gets increasingly sleepy. I hope so. Only a crab really knows.

CAVIARE

If rich readers will promise *never* again to eat *pâté de fois gras*, they can be allowed to eat their fill of caviare with a relatively clear conscience. All sturgeons insist on living free in the Caspian Sea and, despite all efforts, refuse to be farmed. What is more, they live longer than almost anything else we eat. The Beluga, king of the sturgeons, takes twenty years to mature and produce the eggs, which are stripped from its dead body to fill the precious pots. There are dangers of overfishing at present, but generally sturgeons live a long and free life, and fare better than most of the creatures we consume.

FREE-LIVING FISH

All the fish we eat, with the exception of salmon, trout and the occasional turbot, have lived a natural life in river or sea. There are many who fear that this happy situation will not continue for much longer. Selective fishing methods, which left sufficient stocks to replenish the seas, are being replaced by massive plunder. The seabed is being 'hoovered'. Undersized, inedible and unwanted fish and sea creatures are sucked up, dredged up, killed and discarded in their millions. Vast quantities of shoal fish are fed to factory-farmed animals which should be grazing in the fields. In the Pacific, the environmentally unfriendly Japanese are doing their best to wipe out whole species of fish and sea creatures with their twenty-five-mile-long fishing nets. In Europe, we cheerfully disgorge sewage and toxic chemicals into the seas to poison its inhabitants. Oh, what a lovely world! Environmental organizations like Greenpeace and Friends of the Earth, doing their best to fight such abuse of the oceans, deserve support.

However, here we are chiefly concerned with whether it is kinder to eat fish than meat. I believe it is, although I agree with those who maintain that suffering is involved in the production of any animal food.

It would be nice to adhere to the old-fashioned belief that, being 'cold-blooded creatures', fish feel no pain. Codswallop, I'm afraid. Scientific evidence now clearly indicates that, yes, fish do feel pain and also stress. They have a complex, well-developed brain and a central nervous system very similar to our own. Like us they also have stress hormones, which react in the same way as ours when they are faced with life-threatening situations.

It would be nice to think that fish were caught and killed with due care to prevent suffering. Not so. Sea fish meet a variety of most unpleasant ends, as you will discover later in this book.

However, with the exception of those caught in gill-nets, which may take several hours to suffocate, most are killed quickly. Arguably, even the gill-netted fish are not subjected to the prolonged horror endured by so many farm animals, usually suffering very many hours and often days of terror and rough handling on their journeys to far-from-humane slaughterhouses.

In life, no farmed animal or bird experiences the complete freedom to exercise its normal behaviour patterns that is enjoyed by the fish. When environmentally friendly fishing methods are used, legislation designed to preserve stocks will usually also ensure fish a longer life than that of most farm animals. Most fish take at least two or three years to grow to the minimum legal landing size, while poultry are allowed to live only a few weeks, and animals like lambs and pigs for only a few months.

ORGANIC and NEAR-ORGANIC MEATS

Organic farming is most associated in many people's minds with the absence of chemical pesticides and fertilizers, and more natural animal feeds. Less well-known, perhaps, is the emphasis it places on humane methods of rearing farm animals. The system aims at a return to good old-fashioned mixed farming, with animals and crops being rotated to replenish the land in the natural way – the very reverse of the present unsustainable intensive system.

Organic farming deserves your support if you want to see an end to the abuses of factory farming. The Soil Association, which has laid down the rules now followed by most other certified organic farmers as well, insists that all animals (except in just a few specific circumstances) are outdoors during the grazing season. Indoors, they must be given space to move around and the straw bedding so often denied to the poor factory-farmed creatures, which are forced to lie on hard concrete or metal slats.

Much animal suffering stems from the factory farming of creatures in huge herds or flocks. Organic-farming rules insist on smaller groups, which reduces both aggression and infection. In addition to these basics, there are rules covering the welfare of each species.

Critics of organic farming can fairly claim that, perhaps in over-reaction to factory farming, which uses medication to keep animals alive in intolerable conditions, organic farmers sometimes resist medical aids which could be used in the interests of animal welfare. There are some diseases, for instance, which can only be controlled effectively by vaccination. Tetanus is a classic example, being due to a spore-forming organism which can survive in the soil almost indefinitely. However, the organic movement is certainly leading farming in the right direction in its general concern for the countryside and the welfare of both humans and animals.

At present, organic farming is only a fringe area of agriculture. Whether it can expand enough to change, or at least strongly influence, the whole system is up to you. Every time you pay extra to buy the organic product you are making an important vote in the politics of agriculture. Even buying organic vegetables helps animals, indirectly. Booming sales in this area have led supermarkets to seek sources of organic meat, poultry and dairy products.

So far, only a scattering of organic animal products are available at the supermarkets. Seek them out if you care about animals (and healthy food). And when you can't find them, or a *Kind Food Guide* recommended free-range product, be prepared to go to the extra trouble of buying from a small shop or farm. For £2.50, The Soil Association, 86 Colston Street, Bristol BS1 5BB, will send you *A Report and List of Producers of Safe Meat in the UK*. In the section 'Addresses of Home Delivery Services', I have given the addresses of two companies which are prepared to deliver organic meat and poultry to your door: *Ian Miller's Organic Meat* and *Greenway Organic Farming* (pages 139–41).

Some foods carry a label stating that they are produced to Conservation Grade standards. From an animal-welfare point of view, this is just as good as organic, arguably better in some instances. The main difference concerns medication. For instance, most livestock are prone to infection by parasitic worms. Organic standards recommend management practices such as clean grazing and strict hygiene as preventive measures and allow the use of drugs only as a last resort. Under Conservation Grade standards, certain carefully selected drugs may be used as a preventive measure, although the routine use of antibiotics and growth promoters is not allowed.

DOWN YOUR AISLE

An At-a-glance Guide to the Kinder Foods Available at Your Own Favourite Supermarket or Store

MARKS & SPENCER

The best store for, in particular, kindly produced pig products. None of their fresh pork now comes from the cruel systems still widely used elsewhere – and they have introduced free-range bacon and sausages.

Pork	ALL of the fresh pork – chops, steaks, escalopes and joints – on sale at all M & S stores is from the kinder systems of pig rearing, so there is no need to look out for special lines here.
Bacon	The bacon sold at M & S labelled 'Free-Range' is the *only* store or supermarket bacon which I can recommend at time of going to press. Most other big-store bacon is a product of highly intensive methods of pig rearing.
Sausages	M & S is also one of the stores to have pioneered 'the kinder sausage'. Buy the ones labelled 'Free-Range'.

Chickens Free-range chickens, available in all M & S stores, provide a much kinder buy than chicken or chicken products which lack this label.

Turkeys Free-range fresh turkeys are widely available at M & S stores, but only during the Christmas season.

Ducks Just a limited number of their stores sell whole, boned, free-range ducks, from small farms in France.

Geese Again, just a limited number of stores, about thirty of the larger branches, sell traditionally reared free-range geese, which are imported from small mixed farms in France, in the week before Christmas.

Organic milk This is available in many of their branches, and is easily recognizable in its distinctive green carton. Availability is still a problem, so it is not necessarily on the shelves all the year round.

Quiche A number of branches now sell a kinder quiche – quiche lorraine made from free-range eggs, and labelled as such.

TESCO

Outstanding for its wide range of humanely reared free-range poultry from France.

Chickens Tesco have acquired exclusive rights to a special breed of chicken, reared by a cooperative of farmers and allowed to roam freely in a huge forest area in south-west France. Both the natural exercise and the foods they forage to supplement the corn they are fed gives their flesh an 'old-fashioned' flavour and texture.

Turkeys From Easter 1991, Tesco will be taking a big step forward in kind methods of turkey rearing by selling free-range turkeys from the same area in France all the year round. These turkeys grow more slowly than factory-farmed birds and have a considerably longer and better life.

Quail Although the industry is only small-scale, many quail are kept in conditions which incorporate much of the cruelty of the battery-hen and broiler-chicken business. Tesco are now selling quail, again from France, reared by a kinder system.

Pork The line of pork to buy at Tesco is that labelled 'Traditionally Reared Prime Norfolk Pork'. This particular pork comes from new and more humane systems of pig rearing – which will be expanded if customers prove willing to pay the small extra cost.

Sausages Like Marks & Spencer's, Tesco now sell a kinder sausage in their larger stores. They are labelled 'Traditional Pork Sausages' and come from pigs reared in kinder and less intensive systems.

Pork pies Tesco have pioneered the first kind

pork pie! This 'Traditional Pork Pie', as it is labelled, is now available in their major stores and uses meat produced in their kinder 'traditional' rearing systems.

Beef 'Traditionally Reared Prime Beef' from guaranteed grass-grazed cattle is now available in about twenty branches. This is the kinder beef to buy at Tesco.

Dairy products Organic Cheddar and Biobree Organic Brie from France are now available in many stores.

Game Available at larger branches, when in season.

Salmon Fresh wild salmon is available in some branches.

SAFEWAY

This store is playing a major role in encouraging organic farming methods and these more kindly and healthily produced animal foods are increasingly available in their stores in wide variety.

Beef Superb organic beef, labelled as such, is available in a number of branches in the south-east.

Veal Safeway are among the few stores to insist on an 'only British policy' in selling veal. The cruelties allowed in overseas systems are now banned by law in Britain, so British veal is the kindest type to buy.

Chickens Safeway sell Moy Park free-range fresh chickens and also free-range breast fillets and part-boned legs. These products come from a kinder system than the cruel broiler-houses which supply most chicken today – so look out for the 'Free-Range' label at Safeway's.

Turkeys Frozen free-range turkeys are available – but only during the Christmas season.

Dairy products Safeway are particularly good for organic cheeses. Pencarreg (similar to Brie) is available at all branches, as is Cardigan, a hard organic cheese which is useful for cooking. A few of their branches in the West of England sell organic milk, and many Safeway's stores sell Busses Farm Yoghurt – one of the few organic yoghurts which is made with organic milk, not just organic fruit.

Game A variety of game birds, including wild duck in some stores, is available during the season.

Lamb Organically farmed lamb is now available in about twenty branches.

Salmon The Irish Seaspray brand of wild Atlantic smoked salmon is now available in many branches.

Mayonnaise Safeway sell Flora Egg-Free Mayonnaise Dressing in some of their branches, which solves the problem of those battery eggs used in many brands of mayonnaise.

Animal-free fats Many branches also sell Safeway Soya Margarine and Safeway Pure

- Vegetable Margarine, which are both animal-derivative free.

J. SAINSBURY

One of the best stores for veal and venison, and their organic milk is widely available.

Veal	Sainsbury is among the minority of major stores to insist on 'only British veal' policy, which thoroughly deserves your support if you like veal but also care about animals. The cruel methods often used to rear veal calves overseas are now, happily, banned in Britain. But much veal, particularly that served in restaurants, is still imported from such systems.
Venison	Most welfarists believe that the kindest way to kill venison is with a shot, at point-blank range, on their home territory. Sainsbury is the only major store to sell venison killed in the preferred way, and the animals live a very natural life.
Chickens	Most Sainsbury's stores sell free-range chickens, and also leg and breast fillets from free-range birds.
Game	Available, when in season, at larger branches.
Duck	Free-range ducks are available, but only over the Christmas period.
Turkeys	Sainsbury's sell fresh and frozen free-range turkeys, but only at Easter and during the Christmas period.

Dairy products   Half of Sainsbury's stores now sell organic milk in their own-label cartons, and most sell Pencarreg organic cheese. Also available at most branches is Busses Farm Yoghurt – one of the few organic yoghurts to be made with organic milk as well as fruit.

Beef   Sometimes the label 'traditional' at Sainsbury simply refers to the curing method – i.e. 'Traditionally Cured' bacon. However, their label 'Traditional Beef' guarantees that the animal has grazed on pasture during the summer and has not been kept in the undesirable indoor intensive systems.

Salmon   Some branches sell fresh wild salmon.

WAITROSE

Some kinder lines are available at Waitrose, if you select with care. Look for the label 'Traditional'. This is a good store for game.

Game   Frozen pigeon and pheasant are available throughout the year at Waitrose stores, and during the season some branches sell fresh pheasant, partridge, mallard and pigeon.

Turkeys   Frozen free-range turkeys are available all the year round.

Chickens   Moy Park free-range chickens are available at all branches. Service counters also sell 'Farmhouse Chickens' which are more humanely reared than the majority of chickens on sale today, but not as well treated as 'Free-Range' chickens.

Beef
Make sure you buy the Scotch beef sold on meat service counters, or the prepacked beef labelled 'Speciality Beef' at Waitrose, as other prepacked beef sold there comes from zero-grazing units.

Pork
Choose 'Traditional English Pork', as the animals which provide this range are specially reared in kinder, less intensive conditions. Joints, chops, spare ribs, etc., are available at the service meat counters and 'Traditional English Pork' joints, so labelled, are also now available prepacked in selected branches.

Sausages
The kinder sausage is also available – the label to look for is 'Traditional Pork Sausage'.

Salmon
Wild salmon, both whole and in steaks, and wild salmon trout are available in some branches.

ASDA

This is the first of the supermarkets to introduce Conservation Grade meat, selected for them by the Pure Meat Company, which specializes in products from high-welfare systems. Rearing methods are similar to those used in organic farming, but a little more leeway is allowed in the use of selective preventative medications.

Beef
More than fifty Asda branches now

sell beef with the Conservation Grade label. The special range includes joints, steaks, mince and a range of stewing beef.

Lamb Conservation Grade lamb is also available in many Asda stores.

Chickens All Asda stores sell Moy Park free-range chickens, and this year they are also planning to introduce free-range Conservation Grade chickens into some of their branches. All stores now sell 'Farmhouse Chickens', more humanely reared than the majority of chickens on sale, but not as well treated as free-range chickens.

Pork Specially labelled pork from outdoor reared animals kept in more humane systems is also being introduced into many branches this year. Look out for it.

Dairy products Pencarreg and Cardigan organic cheeses are available in some of their West Country branches.

Game Larger branches sell game, when in season.

ICELAND

This chain of frozen-food stores has, of late, shown a commendably 'green' attitude and been quick to introduce more kindly reared animal foods, including organic beef.

Beef Iceland's organic beef is an ideal buy for those seeking the finest in flavour, and organic beef cattle are the least likely to suffer from BSE. They sell joints of topside, 2 lb packs of mince and $\frac{1}{4}$ lb beefburgers in packs of four, all from the specially labelled organic range.

Pork   Under the 'Naturally Reared Prime British Pork' label, they sell a special range of pork – chops, shoulder and leg – from pigs reared in kinder, more extensive systems.

Chickens   All Iceland stores now sell Moy Park free-range chickens.

HOME DELIVERY SERVICES

THESE days, we can buy more humanely reared and healthier meat and poultry even when these aren't on sale in the supermarkets. Ordering can be as quick as picking up a phone and giving a credit-card number. The food will be delivered to your door. The home delivery companies I list below all offer such a service, nationwide.

It costs more to buy from these welfare-minded suppliers, but there is a huge bonus in flavour and peace of mind. Since so many of us are rightly worried about the dangers to human health of factory-farming practices, it can make sense to bulk-order and deep-freeze more naturally produced foods – particularly with products like beefburgers and sausages which are popular with children.

Here are the addresses and some basic details of the companies. Each will happily supply you with a product and price list.

Ian Miller's Organic Meat
Jamesfield Farm, Newburgh, Fife
Tel. 0738 85498
This well-established organic farm has the best of credentials. Their products carry the Soil Association Symbol.

They offer a nationwide twenty-four-hour delivery service of fresh vacuum-packed organic beef and lamb, free-range pork, bacon, chicken and game-shot venison, and make a reasonable delivery charge of £6 in Scotland or £8 in England and Wales, for any quantity of products you care to order.

As this company delivers a range of products useful for a young family (e.g. beefburgers at 35p each, beef sausages at £1.35 per pound), it could be worth getting together with neighbours who are equally worried about feeding their children factory-farmed meat for a regular delivery.

The Pure Meat Company Ltd
Coombe Court Farm, Moretonhampstead, Devon
Tel. 0647 40321
This company is a member of the Guild of Conservation Food Producers which imposes high standards for animal welfare, very similar to those in organic farming. The animals are reared and fed in a healthy, natural way.

The company supplies a wide range of products – beef, veal, pork, lamb, sausages, bacon, ham, Christmas turkeys, poultry and game. They will deliver, overnight, to anywhere in Britain. There is no delivery charge on large orders of 25 lb of meat and over, which can be made up from a wide variety of products. They will also deliver single joints or smaller orders, but there will then be a carriage charge. Phone the number above for their price and product list. You can place your order by telephone, with a credit card.

Greenway Organic Farms
FREEPOST, Edinburgh, Lothian EH1 0AQ
Tel. 031 557 8111
This company specializes in a home delivery service of

organic beef and lamb, from farms certified by the Soil Association, which guarantees high animal-welfare and health standards. They also supply a range of French organic poultry – chicken, duck and guinea-fowl. They will deliver overnight, all over Britain. There is no minimum order, but there is a delivery charge on orders costing less than £100. Again, you can phone for their product and price list and place orders over the telephone, with a credit card.

The Real Meat Company Ltd
East Hill Farm, Heytesbury, Warminster, Wiltshire BA12 0HR
Tel. 0985 40501

This company will deliver additive-free meat from traditionally reared livestock to your door, providing you order at least 12 lb. There is a delivery charge. The order can be made up of any selection of their products, which include sausages, bacon, ham, pork, beef, beefburgers, lamb, chicken, ducks and turkeys. You can order by phone giving your credit card number and, in most cases, the meat can be delivered on the next day.

All farmers supplying the Real Meat Company must adhere to a strict welfare code which cuts out the cruelties so often involved in factory farming. Happily, this extends beyond the farm gate, where so many farmers wash their hands of the fate of their animals. Slaughterhouses are carefully chosen and checked, calves are not sent to market, sheep are not exported live. All animals, except for some of the pigs, which are loose-housed on straw, are free-range.

PART THREE

THE A TO Z OF EDIBLE ANIMALS

THE A TO Z OF EDIBLE ANIMALS

How is it farmed, how is it fished – and is this a system YOU can feel happy about? Here is the first caring person's guide to just about every fish, fowl and edible animal, so that you can make informed choices and live at peace with your food.

ANCHOVIES

Unlike farm animals, most of the fish we eat live a completely free life in their natural environment. Only those particularly prized for their flesh and flavour, like salmon and trout, carp and turbot, command the kind of price that makes fish farming economically viable.

Anchovies, tiny fish which swim in huge shoals in warm seas, come at the opposite end of the economic scale. They can be netted out of the seas in such vast quantities that most of those caught are ground into fish-meal to feed farm animals. However, overfishing of anchovy off the South American coast has shown that the sea is not inexhaustible when fished by today's voracious methods. A few years ago the once-great shoals suddenly and totally disappeared from some areas.

Today, most of the canned anchovy sold in Britain is caught off the coast of Portugal and Morocco, by a traditional small-boat fishing industry. The shoals of anchovy are encircled by nets which are drawn around them to concentrate them into a dense, seething mass. Neither modern nor traditional fishing methods are particularly humane in the way they kill their fish, but most anchovies are likely to die quickly, cramped and suffocated before they are pulled on board.

Since they rose to popularity on the top of the ubiquitous pizza, more of the anchovy catch is used for human food. Before being canned they are marinated in salt for two or three months, which gives them their strong, distinctive flavour.

BEEF CATTLE

Beef rearing encompasses some of the better systems in British farming – and some of the worst. That Sunday joint or pound of mince may have come from an animal which spent its summers suckling from its mother and grazing in the fields. Or it may be the flesh of the unfortunate offspring of a dairy cow which was taken from its mother at a few days of age, never saw green grass, lived out its existence crowded with its kind on comfortless slats and fed on cheap and often bizarre foods, some of which are thought, in the past, to have given rise to BSE, 'mad cow disease'.

Beef buying poses a particularly difficult problem for the shopper concerned with healthy and humane farming methods. In most cases you can't differentiate between the good beef and the bad on the meat counter. Neither can your butcher or supermarket. Beef cattle, unlike most of today's 'farm' animals, are kept in relatively small herds. A herd of a hundred to two hundred would be typical. Meat wholesalers usually make up their bulk supplies by buying in from many small producers, using a variety of different systems, and the intensive and extensive are all mixed up by the time the beef reaches the meat counter.

The labels and sources which ensure grass-grazed beef are described on pages 92–4. Otherwise, any beef you buy could have been reared in any of the following ways:

Suckler Herds: the Best of Beef Rearing

In the past, the vast majority of British cattle raised for beef have been the offspring of dairy cows, but in recent years, due largely to 'milk quota' reductions in dairy herds, there has been a growth in herds kept entirely for beef production. These are known as suckler herds, and these days supply nearly 40 per cent of British beef.

Along with lambs, beef cattle raised in this way are now among the very few farm animals which are not separated from their mothers shortly after birth. Calves and cows graze together for at least one summer. Like dairy cattle, they will usually be kept indoors during the winter months for convenience of feeding and to protect the pasture. Most suckler calves are slaughtered between one and two years of age. Their mothers, not subjected to the milk-production stresses of the dairy cow, may live as long as twenty.

Semi-intensive: the Most Common Beef-rearing System

Most of the calves raised for beef are still supplied by the dairy herds. These young creatures are given a harsh start in life, moved off their farm of origin at about one week of age, often mixed through two or more markets and transported long distances, sometimes the full length of the country. According to one of Britain's leading cattle experts, Professor A. J. F. Webster of Bristol University, 'Such animals are deprived of normal food, water and physical comfort, and are confused, exhausted and exposed to a wide range of infectious organisms of which the most important are the salmonella bacteria. By the

time they reach their rearing unit, they are infected, dehydrated and stressed, and need special care if they are to survive.'

The calves which end up in the traditional beef units will graze in the fields in summer and be confined in barns and farm buildings during winter. Indoor conditions vary from farm to farm. Most farmers will supply their cows with straw for bedding which all animals, particularly such heavy creatures, need for comfort. A minority, however, follow the example of the agricultural research establishments at Liscombe and Stoneleigh, who have encouraged farmers to cut production costs by leaving their cows to lie on concrete slatted floors.

Generally, however, traditionally reared beef cattle do not experience the extremes of cruelty suffered by many of today's most intensively reared farm animals, but neither do they have as natural a life as well-farmed lambs, for instance. They are usually slaughtered at around eighteen months.

Intensive: the Worst System

An estimated 15–20 per cent of British beef cattle are now reared in intensive beef units. These animals will be the offspring of dairy cows, subject to the stresses of market and transportation, described above, and then confined at high stocking density in buildings and yards for the remainder of their lives, usually of just over a year.

The aim is fast growth at low cost, and intensive beef producers tend to work on the assumption that almost any organic matter is worth a try as cheap food. In the past this has included coffee grounds, chicken litter, animal offal and recycled cattle faeces and rumen contents. The feeding of sheep offal, which has now been banned, has been cited as the probable cause of bovine spongiform encephalopathy, the 'mad cow disease', which has rampaged through British cattle herds during recent years, and caused British beef to be banned from many overseas markets.

Like all other intensive rearing systems, intensive beef rearing much increases the incidence of cross-infection among the animals. So many young calves have died of pneumonia that specialist contract-rearing units have been developed to rear calves for their first twelve weeks until they are better able to survive the conditions of the fattening units.

There will be some variation from farm to farm, but many intensively reared cattle are kept on hard slatted floors with no straw or soft material for bedding, little space to move and no outlets for their normal behaviour patterns. High stocking densities lead to frequent aggression, resulting in injury and bruising. Like broiler chickens and turkeys, they often suffer much pain in their unexercised limbs, which are unable to support such a rapidly growing body properly. Even standing up or lying down – the only activity allowed them – is a slow and painful process. A wretched life.

CHICKENS (Table Birds)

Broilers

Packaged and prepared in literally hundreds of different ways, chicken – once reserved for special treats – is now the most popular meat in Britain. Sadly, all those drumsticks, breasts, curries, nuggets and crispy-coated portions come from an industry which has taken intensive farming almost beyond the realms of imagination. Picture, if you can, a vast sea of one hundred thousand chickens crammed together in one windowless shed.

Unless specifically labelled 'free-range', you can be sure that just about all chicken or chicken products in the shops come from the huge intensive broiler industry which has taken the art of producing cheap meat at high speed to the ultimate. In order to do so they have long since ceased to consider chickens as sentient creatures. These days they are usually referred to as 'a crop'.

Most broiler-chicken factories are huge. They can operate on a low-staff, low-cost basis by following this formula: buy day-old chicks which have been specially bred for remarkably rapid growth; pack a 'crop' of ten to twenty thousand (sometimes as many as a hundred thousand) into a shed at maximum density – just over half a square foot of floor space per bird is usual; put growth-promoting antibiotics in their food; leave them there to expand so that there is no longer any spare space, just a solid sea of chickens standing in a bed of what once was litter but now consists mainly of their own droppings; kill and process them at seven weeks.

Broiler chickens live in a twilight world of dimmed lighting. Conditions during the first two or three weeks of their short lives are sterile, but at least there is space to move. From then on, with each week of growth, things will deteriorate.

Bred and fed for hugely abnormal growth, the modern broiler chicken has been turned into one of the fastest growing creatures on earth. The birds' weight will soon increase beyond the support capacity of their own skeletons. Their bodies become too heavy for their legs. Millions of them suffer from painful leg and feet deformities. During the last week of life they can barely move, and scientists who have examined their bodies believe that they spend their final days in constant pain.

The litter is never cleaned out during the lifetime of each 'crop' of birds. As it becomes wet and greasy from their droppings and the decomposing bodies of some of the birds which have died (about 6 per cent fail to survive even the few weeks to slaughter), chickens develop hock burns, the equivalent of bed sores. In some flocks as many as 85 per cent suffer from this painful condition. Others suffer from breast blisters and ulcerated feet. Overcrowding is sometimes so bad that birds trample each other and even die of thirst, unable to reach the water trough.

Not surprisingly, in such conditions, disease and cross-infection flourish. Many broiler chickens are contaminated by *Salmonella enteritidis* and other bacteria by the time they reach the consumer, and the onus is on him/her to render this harmless by making sure that the chicken is fully cooked.

For the broiler chicken, death follows the same merciless mass-production process as life. The chickens are crammed together in crates, often subjected to long journeys, then hung up by their feet for movement by conveyor belt to a far-from-foolproof stunning process. Many birds will reach the automatic knife still conscious. A cruel end to a short and wretched life.

Corn-fed Chickens

The label 'corn-fed', conjuring up the image of a happy little flock of chickens being thrown handfuls of corn by the farmer's wife, can be misleading. Unless also labelled 'free-range', these birds are simply broilers, raised in the same way as those described above. The only difference lies in their feed. Corn is included to give their flesh the distinctive yellow colour.

Free-range Chickens

The spotlight of publicity on the health problems of the poultry industry and the tastelessness of the factory-farmed bird have led to a rapidly growing demand for free-range chickens in recent years. Now free-range chickens and chicken portions are available in almost every major food store.

Large-scale free-range chicken farming, as practised today, is usually far removed from the little flock we like to picture on the old-fashioned mixed farm. But it represents a big step forward from the stinking prison of the broiler-house, and one which deserves to be encouraged.

Details of the kinder alternatives, and where to find them, are on pages 70–72.

COCKLES

A cockle can usually count on being left in bed, in the bays and estuaries around Britain, for a peaceful life of about four or five years. Not valuable enough to be cultivated, it is left alone to grow to edible size. Then, in some coastal areas, it will be gathered in the old traditional way. Pickers go out in small boats and rake the cockles from offshore sandbanks as the tide recedes. In other areas, like the Thames estuary, a less environmentally friendly mechanism has been introduced and they are gathered more speedily by suction dredge.

Cockles are usually cooked/killed in high-pressure steamers. Cooking takes about six minutes. No one really seems to know how long it takes to kill a cockle, but most small sea creatures are thought to die quickly when their body temperature is raised.

COD

You can feel comfortable about the natural life of the cod which, along with other white fish, is fished out of the open sea. Regulations should ensure it at least one to two years of freedom before reaching the minimum legal size for landing. Netting used for the capture of cod is generally of a mesh size large enough to allow the younger fish to escape.

The manner of death of the codfish which finally lands on your plate is much more difficult to determine. Cod are demersal fish, which means they generally live in the bottom few fathoms near the bed of the sea. Those trawled from the depths, as many are, will almost certainly be dead by the time they reach the surface of the water. Death occurs as the swim-bladder expands rapidly in the changing pressure on the way up.

When swimming in pursuit of food, cod can be found anywhere between the sea bottom and the surface, so some will be captured nearer the surface and landed on deck alive. How long they can stay conscious or alive is open to conjecture, but the common practice is to gut fish like cod and haddock immediately. Which, in some cases, must mean while they are still alive.

Yet a different and slower end lies in wait for those cod which are now caught in monofilament gill-netting, which is stretched like an invisible wall in the sea and left there until the fishermen return a day or two later to collect it. Here the cod will become entangled by their gills. Unable to breathe properly, they usually die of suffocation, which can take several hours.

CRABS

The crab which is sold fresh, for salads and sandwiches, has usually enjoyed a reasonably lengthy life in the coastal waters of Britain and been caught by environmentally friendly methods. Fishing legislation requires that his body must have grown to at least four inches before being taken from the water. This ensures a life of four or five years. During that time, the crab will have done a good deal of roaming under the sea. Tagged females, released at Whitby in Yorkshire, have been captured as far as two hundred miles away, on the Scottish coast, just over a year later.

Crabs are still caught by the traditional method of leaving baited pots under the water, arguably the most environmentally friendly of today's fishing methods. The crabs can enter, but can't escape. Fishermen, emptying the pots, can release undersized crabs and other unwanted intruders alive and usually undamaged into the sea. This contrasts with many modern fishing methods which result in a vast indiscriminate killing of undersized and unwanted fish and sea creatures.

Crabs can live in air, as long as they are kept damp and cool, so on board the boats they are packed in boxes lined with wet straw or shavings. Those sold in Britain are usually delivered to processing plants very near the shore, but a growing export trade in live British crabs means that many will die from stress or suffocation before reaching their overseas destination.

The killing of a crab is one of those 'don't know' areas which is particularly complex in the case of crustacea. To us the method employed, which is usually that of drowning the crab in fresh water, appears more humane than the boiling-water death of the lobster. The crab escapes the latter fate because it sheds its claws and often suffers meat deterioration if boiled alive.

There is an instant way of killing crabs. The Universities Federation for Animal Welfare recommends that they should be spiked in their two nerve centres. In practice, however, this requires time and a degree of skill, so fishermen usually resort to the alternative method of leaving them to drown by immersing them in fresh water. This way the crab takes several hours to die. What suffering is involved is unknown. Some scientists suspect that, as the body fluids are diluted, it may gradually become comatose.

CRAYFISH

Crayfish are a freshwater cousin of the lobster. Almost all of those you may be sold, whether small crayfish garnishing a nouvelle cuisine creation or large ones sold on fish counters, will have come from crayfish farms.

Wild crayfish are rare. Our indigenous population was

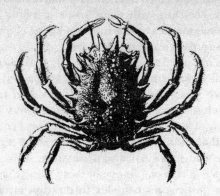

decimated by plague early in the century. A thriving rural industry now supplies the growing demands of the restaurant trade by stocking farm ponds, lakes and gravel pits with faster-growing American crayfish, letting them breed and multiply and then capturing them in traps like lobster-pots.

Among those with a great taste for crayfish are other crayfish. The trick, in farming, lies in getting them to produce more relatives than they eat. There must be sufficient area of banking to allow each crayfish to have a hide, and so bank area largely governs the density of stocking. At the more intensive end of the business some producers use artificially created long narrow ponds for this purpose. Supplementary feeding also encourages the crayfish to live at a higher-than-natural density. Being omnivores they will accept almost any food, from par-boiled potatoes to fish or animal offal. Foods made especially for crayfish are now becoming available.

Crayfish usually reach the desired market size at about eighteen months. They are always sold live. Packed in special boxes with some damp material like grass they can live as long as ten days on their journey to restaurant kitchens.

Like most other shellfish, crayfish are boiled alive. How long they take to die will largely depend on the size. Small crayfish are likely to die in a few seconds, while the larger, almost lobster-sized specimens will suffer the more prolonged death in boiling water that deters many people from eating lobsters.

DAIRY CATTLE

Modern life in the dairy industry is far from being all clover for the cow. True, she will usually spend her summers grazing in the fields, and is not, in that sense, 'factory-farmed'. But by the age of six or seven, after four to five years of milking, her body will be utterly worn out by excessive overwork as a milk machine.

More input, more output is the constant aim of the modern dairy game. By selective breeding and the feeding of concentrates, the cow has been engineered into producing about three times as much milk as her predecessors early in the century. So much milk that Europe has become awash with it. Quotas have had to be imposed to cut back on the vast mountains of milk products being stored at the taxpayers' expense.

Yet still the aim is even *more* milk from each cow. Experiments have recently been carried out in the use of a genetically engineered growth hormone (BST) on some British farms. Injected into the cow each day, this boosts her already hugely abnormal milk product by a further 20 per cent.

And what of the cow? The term 'production disease' has been coined to describe the many painful and distressing conditions which have already arisen as a direct consequence of the post-war drive to produce more milk. Selective breeding for high yields has inevitably led to larger and more pendulous udders than were ever intended by nature. This causes chronic discomfort to the cow and makes her prone to a range of painful infections of the mammary glands. Mastitis is rampant among British dairy herds.

Another consequence of this huge, unnatural udder is that the cow's hind legs have become distorted to accommodate it. This, and long periods of standing on concrete during winter months, have made her inordinately prone to foot ailments, which often cause her excruciating pain. Too-short cubicles, which mean that the cow's hind legs are often standing in moisture and muck, have added to the problem. Inspections of the feet of cull cows at slaughter have revealed that nearly every animal was suffering, or had suffered from, some form of foot damage.

Not surprisingly, since her digestive system, which was designed to deal with grass, is now required to deal with such large quantities of concentrated food, the cow has become prone to acute stomach discomfort and disorder.

The modern dairy cow is expected to give birth each and every year. Those which fail to do so will quickly find themselves diverted into filling beefburgers. Cows are re-mated, usually by artificial insemination, about three months after giving birth, so for most of the year these overworked mothers are pregnant as well as lactating.

It is all too easy to overlook the fate of the calves in weighing up the degree of cruelty involved in dairying. Some will be kept and reared as dairy replacements, others transported to beef-rearing units. Those not suitable for beef may be slaughtered at about two weeks to provide rennet, which is removed from their stomachs and used in the production of many hard cheeses. The worst fate of all, however, lies in store for an estimated

300,000 British dairy calves which are exported each year to endure confinement in the notorious European veal systems which are described on pages 230–32, a system so cruel that it is now banned in Britain.

No young creature is more harshly treated than the dairy calf in present marketing systems, and many will die or become diseased before they reach their destination. Not a lot has changed, says Ruth Harrison, the distinguished farm-animal welfare campaigner, since she wrote this moving description in 1964 in her book *Animal Machines*.

> *The calf is taken, often without feed inside, and bundled into the back of a truck, exposed to the cold and rigour of a market, to the cruelty of some drovers with their hobnailed boots and sticks. Neither the drovers, nor the boys who help them, appear to notice the distress of these young animals, indeed the children follow the men's example of whacking the sides of pens where animals are quietly lying momentarily oblivious of their plight, laughing as they start up again in fear.*
>
> *After the rigours of the market some calves travel hundreds of miles to veal centres in cold, overpacked lorries, or await their turn at the slaughterhouse. Slaughterhouses are not compelled to feed an animal unless they keep it for more than twelve hours.*
>
> *So these gentle little creatures meet their end, a few days after being born, having experienced nothing but hunger and fear in our hands.*

The darker side of the dairy industry is far removed from the carefully promoted image of contented cows nibbling grass and buttercups in green pastures. Organic milk, cheese and yoghurts generally offer a kinder alternative – less overworked cows, and calves (much in demand for rearing as organic beef) less likely to be subjected to markets and export for veal production.

DAIRY SHEEP

Sheep dairying is a growing alternative enterprise in British farming, since British tourists acquired a taste for sheep's milk products on their holidays in Greece. At present there are about two hundred producers, with herds of from fifty to a hundred and fifty animals. It is not as 'small-scale' as goat dairying, but still relatively so compared to other areas of 'farming'.

The sheep used for dairying are special breeds, more prolific and with higher milk yields than sheep raised for meat. Most are less hardy, and will be kept in farm buildings during winter months. But here, in groups on straw, they generally have more space and mobility than cows. Not being quite as 'hard-pushed' as dairy cattle, their productive lives tend to be a little longer. Grass will provide only a small proportion of their food – silage and concentrates the rest.

Most dairy sheep will be mated three times every two years (their pregnancies last for five months). Often they will produce twins or triplets, so a large number of lambs must be disposed of in order to leave milk for human consumption. Sheep and lamb are usually separated soon after birth. The vast majority of lambs are fattened up for four months to be slaughtered for meat. Nearly all will be kept in farm buildings, where they fatten up more quickly than those out at grass. However, in relatively small groups, on straw, they tend to fare better than young animals like pigs, which are often kept in dismal, sterile factories.

DEER

Despite the growth of deer farming in recent years, most venison served and sold in Britain still comes from wild

game. Farmed venison, mainly sold in supermarkets and farm shops, only accounts for about 25 per cent.

Of late, the numbers of wild deer in Britain have increased. Wild herds abound in the Scottish highlands and forested areas of England and there is comfort in the thought that much of the wild meat comes from necessary culls. When deer become too numerous in an area, many animals die a slow, lingering, winter death from starvation. Hence, most animal welfare organizations do not object to culls by trained professional stalkers.

More controversial is the culling of deer as part of a profitable blood-sport business. Deer-stalking is a booming leisure industry in Scotland. Sportsmen are willing to pay large sums to hunt and shoot the animals; the carcasses remain the property of the estate owners and are sold to game dealers.

On the whole, however, deer shooting is well controlled, and trained professionals, able to deliver the *coup de grâce* to wounded animals, usually accompany the sportsmen. Game-shot venison is one of the few meats consumed today which comes from an animal which has lived a free and natural life.

Deer farming, the other source of venison, prides itself on being one of the most 'clean and green' areas of modern farming, and with some justification. But there are worrying signs that some members of the British Deer Farmers' Association are attempting to change things for the worse in the sacred name of faster production and profit.

At present, because they are classed as game, deer can be shot at point-blank range in the field in which they graze. The RSPCA and Compassion in World Farming believe that this is the most humane way to kill these still semi-wild animals – sparing them all the fear and stress of transportation and slaughterhouses. Both farmers and welfarists report that when deer are shot in the field there are no signs of alarm in the herd. Other deer, in close proximity, continue to graze undisturbed.

The method becomes less practical, however, when deer are farmed and slaughtered in large numbers. Some deer are now being sent to slaughterhouses. In the interests of expansion, efficiency and hygiene, although arguably not of the deer, some farmers are pressing for this practice to become more widespread. At present most venison sold in supermarkets (apart from Sainsbury's) are killed at a special deer slaughterhouse in Hertfordshire run by a company called Pelham Venison, who are Britain's largest producers and wholesalers of farmed venison. Here conditions are generally more humane than those at many other slaughterhouses and more thought has been given to preventing suffering and stress. However, many welfarists still consider this to be only second best to field slaughter.

More worrying are the trials which have been carried out in recent years on the intensification of deer farming. At one agricultural college, deer have been kept in sheds and allowed only limited exercise in concrete yards, with the aim of saving costs on field fencing and achieving faster growth for earlier slaughter.

Hopefully, the 'greener' deer farmers will prevail in the current conflict between those who want to keep this area of farming extensive and agribusinessmen who seem to want to introduce intensive methods, just at a time when the error of this approach is being understood in other areas of agriculture.

The best of the deer farmers graze their animals in parkland or wide areas of varied landscape. Many more graze them in paddocks, some reasonably spacious, others questionably limited in size. Like cattle, some deer are kept in farm buildings during winter months, largely to protect the pasture; while others, on more suitable and extensive areas of land, will stay out of doors. Growing calves, born the previous summer, are usually winter-housed on the reasonable grounds that they are less able to cope with bad weather, which kills off many young animals in the wild.

Farm-born calves suckle from their mothers for the first four months – longer on some of the better farms – and are slaughtered at between fifteen and twenty-seven months of age.

DUCKS

Forget that idyllic rural scene of ducks and ducklings waddling through farmyards, foraging in fields, splashing in ponds. Duck rearing today means about half an acre of identical white ducks, some eight thousand in number, just standing together in one big shed.

These days, nearly all ducks sold or served in Britain are factory-farmed. A few large companies, mainly in the east of England, dominate the market. Assume your oven-ready bird or *canard à l'orange* comes from that source unless the shop or menu specifically states 'wild' or 'free-range'.

Duck rearing is now similar to the broiler-chicken business, although not quite so intensive. Conditions are a little better for the birds: they are given more space (about two square feet each), which allows for straw or sawdust to be topped up daily. In a well-run duck unit buildings will be light and airy.

Like the broiler chicken, the modern duck has been bred for high-speed growth. Its weight increases at twice the rate of its predecessor. It is hatched, reared and dispatched in little more than seven weeks. But with a heavier frame and less flesh than the chicken, the duck remains able to support its own weight. Duck producers also tend to have their own slaughterhouses, which spare the birds long stressful journeys.

Though not subjected to as much suffering as the chicken, the modern duck endures a sterile existence. Not for her the instinctive pleasures of bathing, dabbling and splashing for which her webbed feet and well-oiled feathers were made. She is a duck out of water. Just another little meat machine.

DUCK (Wild)

The wild duck, occasionally offered in restaurants and sold in 'high-class' butchers' shops, offers a kinder and more flavourful alternative to the factory-farmed bird. This duck will be the product of a shoot. It is unlikely to have been born and bred in the wild, but will at least have known the pleasures of freedom and water for most of its life.

Traditionally, wildfowlers hide in cover on wetlands and wait for wild birds to fly into their feeding grounds. Much of this kind of shooting still takes place around Britain's coastal waters, but skill and patience are required and the bag is rarely big enough for the commercial market.

Wild ducks sold to the public via the game dealers are generally the product of a much more commercial operation – the driven shoot. Game estates, currently experiencing a boom as part of the corporate leisure industry, sometimes offer a duck shoot as a special attraction during a day's pheasant shooting.

These ducks will usually have spent the first six weeks of their lives in intensive conditions on game farms, but they are easier to rear than pheasants (see pages 192–4) and problems like feather pecking and vent pecking rarely occur. At six weeks they will be released on inland areas of water to spend the remaining three or four months of their lives in comparative freedom. Some fencing will be used, initially, to protect them from predators as they adapt to the wild.

A good deal of controversy currently surrounds game shooting, and traditional sportsmen complain of ducks being driven off the water by dogs and stones on badly run, cash-in-quick estates. But the sporting bodies are taking steps to put their own house in order. When ducks are properly naturalized they can be driven into the air simply by the appearance of a gamekeeper near the water.

Some ducks, of course, will escape the guns. The wisest of these will leave the estate and fly off to become part of Britain's flourishing wild-duck population, benefiting from the extra areas of inland water created as a result of gravel extraction. All in all, and despite drawbacks, the lifestyle of a wild duck offers considerable advantages to the short and dreary existence of a factory-farmed bird.

EELS

Eel farms, keeping as many as 100,000 eels in one warm and smelly tank, were once a popular enterprise in Britain, but in recent years, many ran into economic problems. Few remain. Today's smoked and jellied eels are largely the product of fishing. Often they have lived in fresh water for many years, and have even been known to survive for as long as twenty-five.

The eel lives a most extraordinary life and makes a remarkable journey in order to reach our rivers and shores. Naturalists believe that all eels are born deep in the Sargasso Sea, which lies between Bermuda and Puerto Rico.

It may take two or three years for the eels to reach our coast. Drawn by their instinct to make their way into fresh water, the young creatures, known as elvers, move into bays and estuaries. In late spring, great numbers begin river journeys upstream. It was at this stage that many were caught for eel farms, which were usually located near power stations, for the warm water was found to speed their growth.

The wild eel usually enjoys a long life. It takes seven to ten years to reach sexual maturity, at which stage the eel's belly turns from yellow to silver and it starts the long journey back to the Sargasso Sea. Silver eels move down river in late summer and autumn, mainly by night. This is when most are caught, in nets strung across the rivers.

Eels can stay alive for lengthy periods out of water, as long as their skins are kept wet. Usually they are transported live, in boxes topped with trays of dripping ice.

Unfortunately they are difficult to kill. Even when their heads are chopped off the body continues to move vigorously. The method found most practicable in the industry appears to be particularly cruel and prolonged. Most are part-buried in salt which gradually penetrates the body. This serves the dual purpose of both killing the eels and removing much of the slime. Usually the process lasts for about two hours, although there are suggestions that the eel may be dead after about ten minutes. Eels used for the jellied-eel trade are usually chopped up alive and then boiled.

Eels which escape these cruel fates begin their long return journey, thought to take a year or more, to the Sargasso Sea. Here the female can produce as many as ten million eggs during spawning. It is probable that, shortly afterwards, she dies. Some experts believe that few, if any, of the European eels manage to reach the spawning grounds and that the species is maintained solely by the return of those eels which lived in fresh water in the Americas.

EGGS. See Hens, egg-laying.

FROGS

Frogs' legs are served up in our French-style restaurants at a cruel cost to both the unfortunate creatures and the environment of Third World countries. Frogs play a vital role in protecting crops in rice fields and wetlands from insect pests. India, which used to be the largest exporter, banned the trade after finding that the export revenue was more than offset by the cost of importing pesticides to replace the frogs. Now Bangladesh and Indonesia, who have taken over the trade, face the same problems. Scientists working for the United Nations Food and Agricultural Organization report that crop-devouring insects have increased 'precipitously' in areas where the frogs are caught.

Frog-catching is a peasant-based industry, but one which has nasty long-term consequences to both man and frog. Villagers catch the frogs in rice fields at night, by dazzling them with torches. As many as three hundred may be dropped into one bag and shaken down before the bag is tied at the top. Many of these will already be dead and putrefying in the heat by the time the bag has been transported by bike or bus to the nearest cutting centre.

What awaits the rest is a particularly horrible death. Amphibians die slowly. Short of a motorway, there is no humane way of killing frogs quickly and *en masse*. The live frog is held by its neck and hind legs and thrust against a curved-bladed knife, fixed in a block of wood. It is cut in two across the lower belly.

The still-living front halves are thrown into a heap on the floor to die many minutes – sometimes as long as an hour – later. Campaigners against the trade, at Compassion in World Farming, have horrific pictures of these pathetic half-frogs with gaping mouths, clawing at the air.

Few people who have witnessed this, or the frogs' legs, often thick with flies and sometimes tipped on the floor of the processing factory, retain their taste for this unnecessary food, which costs a hungry world many more calories than it provides.

GEESE

The goose is a singularly intelligent, excitable and active bird which makes it even more than usually ill-suited to the sterile and crowded conditions of indoor rearing. Such personality traits have not spared it from the methods of the intensive farmers. Most geese sold in the supermarkets today are supplied by one big Norfolk production company, which has steadily moved from extensive and semi-intensive methods, in which the geese were allowed to graze on grass for at least part of their lives, to intensive housing. Now most of their geese are confined indoors. They are housed in large sheds, each containing about 8,000 birds, from when they are one day old until slaughter.

Because of their excitable temperaments and wet faeces, geese require more space than turkeys, and good ventilation is necessary because of their tendency to suffer from respiratory problems. However, if you seek a kind alternative to the cruelly abused turkey for Christmas dinner, goose only realistically fits the bill if you buy the free-range bird.

Geese are natural grazers. Under traditional husbandry systems they will obtain most of their food from short-growing grass and weeds. Fortunately, the free-range goose, which has been allowed to follow this natural behaviour pattern, is usually recognizable when sold fresh. Its skin will be a golden-yellowy colour from the carotene in the grass, rather than the near-white of the intensively reared bird. With frozen birds the difference is rather more difficult to detect.

Deprived of the grazing and exploration which normally occupies most of its waking hours, the intensively farmed goose will seek something to occupy its bill and often resorts to what intensive farmers like to refer to as 'vices'. Goslings nibble each other's down, which leads to bare backs and heads, and sometimes results in injury and cannibalism.

The intensively farmed goose, restricted from taking exercise and fed on concentrates, fattens up more quickly than the traditionally reared bird and is usually slaughtered at sixteen weeks. The small size of the goose industry, compared to that of other areas of poultry production, will usually ensure it a quicker death, on the factory premises, than that of hens, which are crammed into boxes and driven for long journeys to slaughter-houses, or turkeys, which are often hung upside-down for an agonizing (and legally allowable) six minutes in the massive pre-Christmas slaughter. Many geese are still slaughtered manually by having their necks broken. Some will be electrically stunned prior to being bled to death.

The only other major producer, E. F. Shingfield & Sons, also in Norfolk, practises semi-intensive rearing methods. The birds have access to either straw yards or areas of grass during the summer months. The limited areas of grass – a thousand birds in a pen of about 50 square yards – allows the bird at least some grazing.

A few free-range geese are a feature of many farms and a small number of specialist producers follow traditional grazing methods with as many as two thousand geese, which are mainly offered for sale in the Christmas season.

GEESE (and DUCKS), FORCE-FED (for Foie Gras and Pâté de Foie Gras)

Foie gras and *pâté de foie gras* are produced from the crammed, distended livers of force-fed geese and ducks. Torture would be the accurate word to use in describing the process by which this delicacy is obtained. In the case of the goose it involves cramming six pounds of maize down the bird's throat each day.

Such extreme cruelty is rightly banned in Britain. But

millions of geese and ducks are being force-fed in France, and the product is imported for sale in our expensive grocers and restaurants.

In France, *foie gras* production is still largely a traditional industry, but now new mechanized techniques are also being used to speed up the rate of force-feeding.

The animal-welfare organization, Compassion in World Farming, has researched the methods used to force-feed the goose (clearly, the process for ducks is similar) and the facts speak for themselves:

> **Traditional Method:** *The grandmother of the household, who keeps her goose in a box, does the feeding three or four times a day. She takes it out of the box and kneeling astride the goose, pushes a funnel down its throat, pours in the warm cooked mash and packs it down the funnel with a wooden pusher. The food is far in excess of what the goose would normally eat. It distends the body, and the overloaded liver starts to swell.*
>
> *Force-feeding is started at four months old. Up to that time the geese have been reared on grass, ranging freely. During force-feeding, which lasts three to four weeks, the goose increases in weight by 61 per cent but the liver increases in weight by 371 per cent. All exercise is forbidden as this would allow some of the liver-fat to be 'burned off'.*
>
> *As the liver swells, breathing becomes difficult and shallow. It may take five hours to feed sixty geese this way. The birds would not be able to stand transport and so are bled to death on the farm.*
>
> **Mechanized Method:** *This involves the use of a machine fitted with an auger and a foot-pedal. The*

*goose is put into a restraining brace which holds its
wings tight to the body and stretches its neck. A funnel
tube enters the throat and a spring clip latches around
behind the skull to prevent the goose moving. The bird
cannot close its throat and cooked maize is pressed into
its gullet. Both the operator's hands are free to massage
the food down the throat.*

*At some production units an elastic band is placed
around the bird's neck to prevent it retching up the
food. Each is given about 600 g of food in the first
week of force-feeding, 1,000 g in the second week
and thereafter the amount increases to 1,300 g per
day (3 lb) and eventually to 3,000 g (6½ lb) before
slaughter.*

GOATS

Goats' milk products are a very recently acquired taste
in Britain. Hence, the majority of British goats are still
kept in a comfortingly traditional way, in small units of
just two to ten animals. Many goat keepers are amateur
enthusiasts or smallholders who sell their cheese and
yoghurt in local shops or at the farm gate.

But sales are expanding, and as farms look for diversification the pressure is on for larger goat farms and more
intensive methods of production. There has been an
increase, of late, in herds of between two hundred and
five hundred animals. Here the goats usually live all or
most of their lives indoors, but generally in more humane
conditions than is the lot of many other intensively
farmed animals. Usually they are housed in groups, on
straw and with sufficient space to walk around. Goats
are much easier to keep clean and comfortable than
cattle, for obvious reasons.

Some of the kinder keepers of these larger herds allow
them out for periods of exercise in fields or yards. But

goats are not 'cost-effective' grazers, like sheep, so, unless the consumer is choosy, their future seems to lie in the boredom of the farm building. Generally, however, the well-run intensive goat farm presents a peaceful picture – well removed from the horrors of the hen or pig factory.

Where the crunch comes, for the kind consumer, is in the fate of the male kids. Although most goats will produce milk for two years after giving birth, the general practice on the larger farms is to mate them yearly. There is no real market for male goats in Britain. Only the Muslim community has a traditional taste for their meat. Those reared on to supply it will, in all likelihood, be killed by halal slaughter, which usually involves having their throats cut while still fully conscious, and being bled to death.

The majority of kids will be killed shortly after birth. Welfare organizations advocate that this should be done by barbiturate injection, but commercial farmers are rarely prepared to pay the £8–10 vet's fee for each kid.

Some send them to slaughterhouses, at a few days old. Others resort to a variety of do-it-yourself methods, which include gassing, shooting or a blow to the head. Clearly the fate of the kids and that of their mothers, when they come to the end of their productive days, is the area to investigate when buying goats' milk products from a local producer. The least caring of goat farmers are those who send their animals off to unknown fates, either at uninvestigated slaughterhouses, or – worse still – to markets. Generally, the larger-scale goat farmer is the more likely to seek financial return from his animals in the form of meat sales, and the small one more likely to put a priority on the most humane killing method. There are, of course, exceptions in each case.

GROUSE

Unlike pheasant or partridge, red grouse, the most common of the grouse species in Britain, cannot be reared successfully on game farms. Wise enough not to thrive on such treatment, they live a completely natural life – albeit a very short one. Any you may be sold or served will have been born free and finished off by a sportsman's shotgun.

Born in April or May on the moorland sporting estates of the north, this ground-nesting bird has little to grouse about in its early relationship with man. The moorland gamekeeper acts as its protector and purveyor of fine food. Many of the foxes and crows, which would normally take many of the eggs and young, are exterminated. Care is taken to ensure that the heather, which provides 95 per cent of the birds' diet, remains vigorous. Strip burning is arranged to ensure a good supply of tasty new shoots. Sheep are not allowed to overgraze.

This idyllic relationship between man and grouse comes to an abrupt end on the Twelfth of August.

Most grouse will be just three or four months old when driven by beaters to the line of butts which provide concealment for the guns. The most fortunate of the grouse will be killed in the air. Many will flutter to the ground wounded, to be retrieved by dogs and finished off by the gamekeepers. Driven grouse shooting in Britain is still the most prestigious form of bird shooting in the world, so at least shoots are well organized and the niceties of sportsmanship observed.

Complaints of cruelty mainly involve the predators. Nature-lovers protest about the wholesale slaughter of foxes and other animals and birds. Often a dead sheep will be buried on the moors as bait, surrounded by wire snares which, if badly set, can cause severe and prolonged suffering to trapped animals.

Grouse shooters counter with environmental claims. Were it not for their sport, even more of the northern heather uplands – the habitat of many wild birds and the last stronghold of some endangered species – would be planted with those dreary rows of alien firs. And the red grouse, like its relative the black grouse, which is now in serious decline, would become yet another victim of the horrors of post-war agricultural policy. All of which seems a sad reflection on modern man.

All in all, however, the short but happy life of the grouse is better than that of farm-reared game – and sheer heaven compared to the horrors endured by the hen.

GUINEA-FOWL
Some keepers like to keep a few guinea-fowl on shooting estates, but these are rarely the birds that end up on the restaurant menu. The roast guinea-fowl you are served is almost certainly a factory-farmed bird. Its life and death follow a similar pattern – sad and short – to that of the broiler chicken or duck.

Guinea-fowl are subtropical birds. They lack the hardiness of the pheasant in coping with the British winter, and are not generally reared or shot as game in this country. What wins a fortunate few their freer lifestyle is their gamekeeper-friendly trait of perching high in trees and sounding loud warnings of approaching predators or poachers.

No trees, no grass, not even a glimpse of sky for the rest. By EEC regulations, guinea-fowl are classed as poultry and are reared indoors, in a similar way, though with more space. Most of those sold in Britain are reared on one specialist factory farm in Norfolk. Here they live together in large numbers in sheds. Like chickens they have been bred to reach marketing size in just eight weeks, and share their conveyor-belt death at poultry-processing plants.

A few are farmed in Britain by free-range methods. Typically, a farmer's wife will keep a small flock as an additional source of income. But before making a farm-gate purchase, see for yourself that the birds really are free-range. Those confined in dark and dirty sheds (as sometimes happens in small-scale production) can fare even worse than those in the more controlled conditions of larger units. Small is not always beautiful.

HADDOCK

The life and death of the haddock is very similar to that of the cod, described on pages 153–4. Usually it will have lived in the sea for a minimum of one to two years before reaching commercial landing size.

HALIBUT

By far the largest of the flatfish, the halibut doesn't grow or reproduce itself fast enough to survive modern fishing methods. Few are caught, these days. Those which do appear on the menu or fish-counter have been trawled as part of a mixed catch of fish. They are usually landed live and gutted immediately like other flatfish.

HARE

Until recently, hares tended to be regarded by country-men as farmland pests. Now, as estate owners cash in on the growing hordes of humans rushing to the countryside in search of something to shoot, the hare is becoming a valuable sporting quarry. On shooting estates, as many as 60 per cent of the hare population may be shot on spring shoots. These are the creatures that will find their way on to the restaurant menu, via the game dealer, or be offered for sale in some supermarkets or in what are known as 'high-class' butchers' shops.

For the hare, this at least means a free life and hopefully a quick death. But in recent years the hare population has suffered a serious decline in numbers in many parts of the country and there are worries about the species becoming endangered. The British Field Sports Society is currently funding the Hare Conservation Project, which is looking into the effects of coursing and shooting.

The cruelties of hare coursing, in which hares are

driven in front of two dogs and often torn apart in a tug-of-war between them, are well known and abhorred by animal lovers. So too is hare-hunting by packs of hounds. But these activities account for considerably fewer animals than shooting, and their mangled victims are unlikely to end up in fit condition to be sold as food.

HENS, EGG-LAYING

Battery System
More than 80 per cent of the eggs sold in Britain are laid by hens caged for life in conditions of extreme and unquestionable cruelty, in what is known as the battery system. These eggs, often labelled 'farm fresh' or 'country fresh', are produced in huge factories which often house as many as 100,000 birds in tier upon tier of cages in each building.

When the battery cage system was introduced in the 1950s, one hen was kept in each cage. Then another was put in to join it, gradually followed by a third, fourth and fifth. At the same time, the size of the cage was being reduced.

Today's typical battery cage measures 18 × 20 in, and houses five laying hens for life.

Under British law, it would be a criminal offence to allow a pet bird to be kept under such cramped conditions, or anything approaching them. The law specifies that a caged bird must be given at least the space to spread its wings. The egg industry is given special exemption from this law.

Independent authorities have repeatedly investigated and condemned the battery system. The European Parliament and the British House of Commons Agricultural Committee have each recommended that it be phased out. Top veterinary scientists have produced sufficient hard evidence of suffering to justify a ban. But, so far, only Switzerland and Sweden have overruled the powerful vested interests and passed laws which will outlaw cages in the near future. The proposed European phase-out has been watered down into meaningless legislation on cage size, which does not even increase the space currently allowed to battery hens in Britain.

For the egg industry, the battery system provides a very cheap and almost fully automated method of producing eggs. Hence their grim determination to hold on to their favourite 'farming' method.

No other egg production system can be run with such little skill and so few staff. Just one or two workers can oversee about 100,000 hens. Food is supplied and excrement removed by conveyor belt. Skilled stockmanship is rarely necessary. Once placed inside her cage the hen will remain there until worn out and ready for slaughter, usually about a year later. Now, new detector machines are even taking over the task of locating the bodies of hens which drop dead in the cage from suffering and stress.

The cost savings of this sytem have been made possible by treating the hen itself as a machine and totally ignoring its needs.

No factory-farmed creature is more deprived. The battery hen is not allowed the ground under its feet nor the air above its head. It must stand and crouch perpetually on harsh wire, which often gives rise to chronically painful foot conditions. Some hens move their feet constantly, in a futile quest for comfort. Others become locked in a stationary position, their claws, grown long through lack of normal friction, permanently curled round the wire on which they stand. The roof of the cage is so low that the hen cannot stretch its head upright, in a normal position, but must hold it permanently bowed.

Of the many sufferings inflicted on the battery hen, experts suspect that the deprivation of a suitable nest or box for egg laying is probably the worst torture. Nobel prizewinner Konrad Lorenz, an expert in animal behaviour, gave the following description:

> *For the person who knows something about animals it is truly heart-rending to watch how a chicken tries again and again to crawl beneath her fellow cage-mates, to search there in vain for cover. Under these circumstances, hens will undoubtedly hold back their eggs for as long as possible. Their instinctive reluctance to lay eggs amidst the crowd of cage-mates is certainly as great as the one of civilized people to defecate in an analogous situation.*

Recent scientific research at Edinburgh and at Oxford University has confirmed that hens have such compelling behavioural needs for nest-boxes that they are even willing to run the gauntlet of water-filled foot baths, unpleasant blasts of air or weighted swing doors, or squeeze through small gaps (something they particularly dislike) in order to reach them.

The need to peck – not just for food, but in order to explore and examine – is another strong instinct. Hens use their beaks as puppies use their teeth, to examine everything that attracts their attention. Kept in a natural way they would spend about 60 per cent of their waking hours pecking and scratching around. In the cage, once they have eaten their fill, they have nothing to peck or explore but each other. Particular problems arise after eggs have been laid and the hen's vent area becomes red and moist, attracting the natural curiosity of other birds. Vent-pecking results in damage to many birds – even death.

Lack of litter for dust-bathing is another major deprivation. It has been compared to keeping a prisoner in a cell without any washing facilities. Eating, drinking and egg laying are the only activities available to the battery hen during its seventeen-hour 'day', induced by artificial lighting, and even these are stressful because of the close proximity of the other birds.

The manner in which battery hens are removed from their cages prior to being killed is no less harsh than the manner in which they are kept. There are many reports of the 'snapping noises' of bones – thin and brittle – which can be clearly heard above the din of the terrified hens as they are pulled from their cages by their legs. Further injuries are inflicted as the birds are crammed into crates. Dislocated hips and severe bruising are common. Many of the crated hens will experience long journeys of a day or more to their slaughter, and dozens of birds in every lorry-load will die of injury, shock or suffocation. Cargoes of birds arriving at processing plants in the late afternoon may, quite legally, be left on the lorry in their crates until the next morning.

In the slaughterhouse, the birds are shackled upside-down by their feet. Research by Drs N. G. Gregory and L. J. Wilkins at Bristol's Institute of Food Research has revealed that 29 per cent will have broken bones – most caused by catching and shackling, but some of long standing – by the time their heads fall into the electric waterbath stunner. Legally, all hens must be rendered unconscious before their necks are cut, but the force of the electric shock shatters already brittle bones, providing the industry with a problem of bone splinters in the meat. A widely adopted 'solution' is to reduce the voltage of the stunner, which results in a vast number of hens meeting the knife fully conscious.

The flesh of the battery hen is in no fit condition to be served up in slices and portions. It is used, instead, in products which require meat of lesser quality – chicken soups, pastes, pies, stock cubes, pet foods and baby foods.

Barn-egg Systems

Aware of growing opposition among the public to the cruelties of the battery cage, the poultry industry has been developing alternative intensive methods of egg production. The method which has so far proved most popular among producers is the perchery system. Eggs produced in this way are sold as 'barn' or 'perchery' eggs.

Hens in the perchery system are kept indoors, but not caged. They are housed at very high density, but tiers of raised perches allow them to make use of the vertical space in the building. From the producer's point of view this has the advantage of allowing almost as many hens to be kept in a given area as the battery-cage unit.

The birds derive some advantages. Most important is the provision of nest-boxes into which they can retire to lay their eggs. There is space for a little more movement and a more comfortable base for their feet. In some, although not all, percheries an area of litter is provided on the floor for dust-bathing.

However, the very high stocking density which EEC marketing regulations allow in percheries cause other severe welfare problems for the birds. In the dense mêlée, many break their breastbones, and cannibalism breaks out in some flocks. Those kept in a perchery for a lengthy period can present a wretched sight, pecked almost bald of feathers. In their attempts to prevent this problem, producers often resort to beak trimming – cutting through the end of the upper mandible and placing the lower beak against a red-hot blade. Research by Dr Michael Gentle and colleagues, in Edinburgh, indicates that this process is not only immediately painful but may well result in prolonged or even chronic pain.

The perchery system has been welcomed as a move in the right direction – away from the battery cage – by welfarists. But not until stocking levels are much reduced could it provide a humane way of keeping laying hens. Very important, also, is the design of the house so that timid birds do not have to cross 'hostile' territory to reach food and water, nest-box and scratching area, etc. The RSPCA, in conjunction with farmers, scientists and Ministry of Agriculture experts, is currently developing practical guidelines for the more humane keeping of laying hens, which, it is hoped, will not only be identifiable by the consumer but will be widely accepted by the industry.

Free-range Systems

These days the label 'free-range' is given to eggs produced by a multitude of methods. Some are small-scale and ideal. Others are bigger and more questionable. All offer at least some improvement on other systems widely practised at present.

The rapidly increasing sales of free-range eggs in recent years has done much to convince the supermarkets that shoppers are prepared to pay a little more for foods from kinder systems.

Hens producing 'free-range' eggs are ensured certain minimum conditions of space and freedom, by EEC law. These include continuous day-time access to open-air runs, where the ground must be mainly covered by vegetation. There is a maximum outdoor stocking density of approximately 400 hens per acre. Indoors, perches, nest-boxes and litter must be provided. So far, so good.

But many of the large production units for free-range eggs are far from idyllic. Often, one large central house is provided for a flock of four thousand hens or more. Inside they may have no more space than battery or perchery hens. In theory, of course, they can always go outdoors, but in practice many birds stay permanently indoors in some of these buildings. This may be because they have difficulty in finding exits, or fear more dominant birds or the conditions outdoors. (Anxious to keep them warm, which cuts down food intake, some producers put only small exit holes in the building.) Hens are reluctant to venture far without some cover from bushes or tall vegetation; they have a strong instinct to hide from predators in the sky. Often they will cluster near the hen-house, in the flat fields which are usually the only outdoor habitat on free-range farms. Often hens in these over-large free-range units are subjected to 'beak trimming'.

Small flocks are obviously better. The best large-scale egg producers house their hens in modern movable buildings, each housing around three hundred birds. And the little local egg producer still exists in rural and semi-rural areas, allowing the purchaser to see for himself that the hens are well-feathered and pecking around busily in ample space and vegetation. Many of the problems in egg production arise from keeping hens together in huge numbers, which does not allow them to establish a natural pecking order which would prevent aggression, so small local producers have a decided advantage in the humane production of eggs.

HERRINGS

Only a minority of the herrings fished out of the sea end up as kippers or other foods for humans. Most are used to feed other creatures – pets, factory-farmed animals, farmed fish!

Herrings congregate in huge shoals near the surface in coastal waters. Here they are fished on a single species basis. The usual netting method, known as purse seining, is to encircle a section of the shoal, and then draw the netting in so that the fish are concentrated tightly together in a netting bag. Most will be near dead from shock or suffocation by the time they reach the deck and will expire quickly.

Herrings escape the more lingering death of gill netting, because these walls of mesh, left floating in the waters off our coasts, have a wide mesh which allows most small fish to escape. They are not gutted on deck, like white fish, because of the impracticality of coping with such large numbers.

Most of the herring which are netted will have lived in the sea for three years or more. The younger fish tend to congregate in inshore 'nursery grounds', which are largely protected from fishing.

The presence of great shoals of herrings in any coastal area is unpredictable. Due to climatic fluctuations and other unknown factors they may suddenly disappear from an area and not return for several years. Conservation measures have to be introduced from time to time to prevent overfishing. In the 1970s a five-year ban had to be imposed on the herring fisheries of Europe to allow the much depleted stocks to recover. These days the catching of herring in certain areas may be prohibited at certain times of year, or the use of some types of gear may be prohibited in special areas. Sophisticated modern scanning methods make the herring shoals easy to locate, and without some protection their numbers could decline rapidly again.

LOBSTERS

Much to the frustration of the fish industry, the lobster still lives free in the sea. Attempts to farm it for its valuable flesh fall foul of one insurmountable problem: lobsters are highly aggressive. So much so that even tiny infant lobsters will quickly kill or injure each other when kept in captive groups. Hence, each one must be penned off separately – a costly system which has not proved economically viable.

This is bad news for the shellfish industry. Under controlled conditions the lobster's growth could be speeded to bring it to marketable size in just two years. But it is very good news for the lobster, left free to roam the sea for a good five years before reaching the minimum legal size for landing.

Lobsters are normally caught in the traditional baited lobster pots, the most environmentally friendly of today's fishing methods. Undersized lobsters, and other un-wanted intruders, can be returned undamaged to the sea, not dumped back dead, as happens with many other fishing methods.

You can feel happy about the lobster's life. Its death is what rightly troubles many people. Able to live up to forty-eight hours, or longer, if kept damp and cool after being taken from the sea, it is usually killed and cooked by being boiled alive.

Little scientific research has been conducted into the pain potential of crustacea, but what evidence there is clearly indicates that this mode of death is as cruel as it sounds. Lobsters have complex nervous systems. Viewed under the microscope, the actual nerve cells appear very similar to our own. And lobsters will respond immediately and vigorously to noxious stimuli. Clearly they should be given the benefit of what little doubt exists about their ability to suffer pain.

The quickest, and therefore the most humane, way to kill a lobster is to split it from head to tail, down the middle line, with a single blow with a sharp knife or cleaver. Obviously this requires skill. The expedient method of dropping it in boiling water results in a more prolonged death.

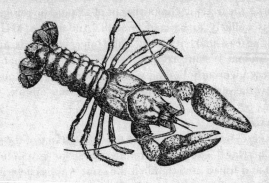

How long the lobster takes to die this way is a subject of some conjecture. Some suggest as short a time as twenty seconds. (Still a long time if you are being boiled alive!) But the observations of a research scientist Dr John Baker, at Oxford University, indicate that it could be a good deal longer:

> *If a lobster is in full vigour at the moment of insertion into boiling water, it struggles violently before it appears to lapse into passivity after about two minutes; uncoordinated jerks of the limbs may be seen five minutes or more after insertion.*

Lobsters which have been kept alive out of water for some time, in fishmongers and restaurant kitchens, become less active and give less vigorous responses. This does not indicate, as Dr Baker points out, that they necessarily die more quickly or feel less pain.

For those not adept with the meat cleaver, and insistent on cooking lobster, there are some indications that fast-freezing offers the lobster a less cruel death. It should be left in a deep-freeze cabinet, at minus 20 °C for two hours – the freezing compartment of a domestic refrigerator is unlikely to be cold enough. And if you MUST boil, at least make it quick. The Universities Federation for Animal Welfare recommends using a large quantity of very vigorously boiling water and holding the lobster below the surface, with tongs, for at least one minute.

MACKEREL

Mackerel swim in large shoals near the surface of the sea, like herrings. They, too, are often used for farm-animal food and fished in very much the same way, as described on pages 184–5. Shoal fish like this die particularly quickly out of water, and are usually dead when landed on deck.

MILK. See Dairy cattle.

MONKFISH

Highly prized by the French, and highly priced when you find it in British shops, the monkfish is a very superior and peculiar fish, with flesh almost as firm as that of a lobster. It has a huge head, much bigger than the remainder of its body, from the top of which projects what looks remarkably like a fishing-rod.

Like all anglers, the monkfish plays a waiting game. It lies still, on the ocean bed, its 'fishing-rod' waving in the water to attract the curiosity of smaller prey. Then – snap! – its huge mouth closes.

When the monkfish gets fished itself, it is usually as part of a mixed catch, trawled from the bottom of the sea. On deck, it usually meets a quick end by being chopped in two. Only monkfish tails are marketed; the bony head is of no commercial value.

MUSSELS

These days, most of the mussels that end up in the *moules marinières* have been cultivated, but by what might be described as a semi-natural process. This largely consists of moving them around in the sea. Infant mussels are lifted from their natural beds and deposited in sheltered coastal areas where they are less likely to be washed out to sea by winter storms.

Once settled, mussels aren't inclined to move around. Some are encouraged (held in place, at first, by what looks like a nylon stocking) to attach themselves to ropes suspended under rafts. Hanging in the water, like this, they are less likely to become gritty than those grown in beds and harvested by dredging or raking. It takes two or three years for them to grow to edible size. They feed themselves by filtering vast quantities of sea water for plankton.

Mussels, kept cool and damp, can stay alive for as long as a week after removal from the sea, by tightly closing their shells to maintain their own micro-environment. They are sold live, and cooked and killed by steaming.

Cooking can take four to five minutes, but the mussel can be assumed to die sooner – as soon as the heat raises its body temperature to 30 °C. The shell opening is a mechanical process which occurs after death.

OCTOPUS

Octopuses are considered to be the most intelligent of all invertebrate creatures and can be taught to do tricks. Scientific tests indicate that they have some capacity to reason, and the ability to choose and remember. They can learn to find their way out of a maze and to differentiate between objects of different shapes and sizes.

Another unusual feature of this extraordinary creature

is its well-developed eyes, very similar to our own. Sadly, this can cause them suffering. Octopuses are often used in laboratory eye experiments and, as vivisection laws only apply to vertebrates, they have no protection.

Although thought of as a warm-sea creature, the octopus is widely distributed in most of the world's seas. Some are caught in our own coastal waters, but they will be relatively small, with a body about the size of a tennis ball and tentacles about a foot long. Most octopuses served up in British restaurants are imported from overseas. The biggest catchers and consumers are the Japanese.

As befits such an unusual creature, the octopus is captured by some unusual methods. The discovery that they were often found in old amphorae, recovered from the Mediterranean Sea, has inspired fishermen to place similar-shaped pots of unglazed clay on the sea bed, or dangle rows of them on lines, as octopus-tempting dark hideaways. The octopuses obligingly climb in and can easily be removed from the sea – ready potted, as it were. In other parts of the world, native divers pull them out of their holes, by hand. Most, however, are caught by trawling.

On board fishing boats, octopuses prove more resilient than their quickly expiring relative, the squid. And often considerably more quick-thinking. Octopuses which have been brought out of the sea, up the side of the boat, and put into a tank of water have often climbed out of the tank, down the side of the boat and into the sea again. Who can blame them?

OYSTERS

Most oysters are now artificially cultivated – but not, one suspects, in a way which need cause oyster or eater too much concern. Natural native oysters, recognizable by their roundish shape and flat tops, are still cultivated or fished from around the coasts of Britain, as they have been since Roman times. But over-fishing, pollution and, in recent years, a pest problem, have reduced their numbers. Like the whelk (page 234), they have suffered from a poison used in the paint for boats' hulls which diffuses in the water.

More common now are the Pacific oysters. These are more elongated in shape and more popular with oyster farmers because they reach edible size in two years, less than half the time it takes the native oyster. Pacific oysters will grow in our chilly British waters, but will not reproduce here. Hence, oyster farmers spawn and rear them in warm water, before suspending them in plastic nets and trays to filter-feed themselves in the sea.

As most people are aware, oysters are eaten alive when served in restaurants. But so, it must be confessed, are most oysters which are born in the sea. One oyster can produce as many as a million offspring in one spawning, out of which only two or three might survive in the highly predatory underwater environment.

PARTRIDGES

In recent years, game farmers have tried rearing partridges entirely for the table – keeping them in intensive or semi-intensive conditions from birth to death. Happily for the partridge, they couldn't compete with all the cheap game-shot birds on the market.

That roast partridge on the menu will be a by-product of the modern shooting bonanza. Almost certainly it was hatched and reared on a game farm, kept there for several weeks and then gradually released for a taste of freedom on the game estates. Often only a very small taste! The partridge season opens on 1 September, about a month ahead of the pheasant season. There are fewer birds available, and the estate owners, cashing in on the current boom, are anxious to get as many birds in the air as quickly as possible for their clients. The farm-reared partridge's life will last for only four months if it is an early victim. Only about half of those released are shot, so many last longer.

The life of the modern game bird is described in detail in the account of that mass-produced target for corporate sport, the pheasant. Partridges lead a similar life, but fewer are reared. This means that they are usually kept in smaller groups on the game farms and are less likely to suffer from aggression.

About a fifth of the partridges shot in Britain are truly wild birds and these, too, find their way to the butchers' shops via the game dealer.

PHEASANTS

'More like battery hens than pheasants ... flying so thick and low you could bag a brace with a cricket bat!' Comments like these, peppering the pages of the sporting press, testify to what some would call the sad decline of the sport of pheasant shooting. Nevertheless, such are the farming practices of our time that the pheasant sold in shop or restaurant offers a kinder choice than most other birds. At least half of its short life will have been spent in a natural environment.

Once the preserve of the gentry, pheasant shooting has suffered the rude shock of becoming a thriving business in the rapidly expanding leisure market. Today's executioner is more likely to be middle management, enjoying a corporate day out, than a double-barrelled colonel of the old brigade. This is not altogether good news for the bird.

The wild pheasant population has declined due to intensive agriculture, so in order to satisfy the huge demand for birds to kill, a large proportion of pheasant chicks are now reared intensively on game farms. Most will live there, in units of a hundred to five hundred, for their first six weeks. Here, the usual problems of keeping birds in confinement at high density can arise. With their fundamental urge to peck unsatisfied, the poults (young birds) often resort to feather-pecking and cannibalism.

Some game farmers employ the preventive method of shortening the upper mandible of the bird's beak. Recent research on poultry by the Agricultural Food Research Council proves that it is a painful process for birds. The alternative method, employed on many game farms, involves fixing a semicircular piece of plastic around the upper mandible to stop the beak closing completely. This appears to be more humane.

At around six weeks the pheasant's life takes a turn for the better. It will be released – often at first into wired-off areas – in the woodland thickets of game reserves. Flight feathers are clipped back (this is not thought to cause pain) to keep the pheasants in these predator-protected areas for two or three weeks until they adapt to the wild. When their feathers have regrown sufficiently the young birds leave the pens of their own accord and start the final free-living phase of their lives.

Sporting traditions require that reared pheasants be given at least twelve weeks of freedom to acquire the behavioural characteristics of wild birds, before becoming targets. Businessmen, cashing in on the popularity of shooting, have less time than the old-style sportsman for such niceties.

A clear idea of the kind of abuses that have crept in is provided by a code of practice recently drawn up by the Game Conservancy and the major British game shooting organizations. The guidelines, unfortunately not enforceable, suggest that no birds be released after the start of the shooting season, nor shot until fully adult and adapted to the wild. They also advise against birds being caught up during the shooting season and re-released elsewhere, and being released into areas in such density that they suffer in health and damage the environment.

One fortunate outcome of the pheasant-shooting boom is a profusion of cheap birds for the market which has ruled out the possibility, on economic grounds, of intensive rearing from birth to death. The participants get their fun with the gun, and are allowed to keep only a brace of birds. The remainder find their way into shops, supermarkets and restaurants via the game dealer.

PIGEONS

The pigeon in the pie was almost certainly a woodpigeon, shot in the cause of what some would describe as 'pest control' and others as 'country sport'. There are an estimated ten million woodpigeons in Britain. Far too many in the view of farmers, who complain of damage to crops and welcome the countrymen who like to shoot the birds.

Most pigeons are shot while feeding on freshly sown seeds or over growing crops. Artificial decoys are often used to attract them. Other shoots are arranged in the evenings, as the pigeons flock into their woodland roosts. There is no closed season. Pigeons are shot at any time of the year, including the protracted breeding season, and nearly all of those killed will be sold as food.

The League Against Cruel Sports considers shooting to be a basically ineffective means of controlling woodpigeons and are opposed to it, except when limited shooting is used to reinforce deterrence. But, in the catalogue of edible birds, the wild life (and – with luck – quick death) of the woodpigeon is one of bliss, compared to those of most of its feathered friends.

PIGS

The pig is considered by experts to be as intelligent as the dog. A House of Commons Agricultural Committee Report, in 1981, described it as 'a naturally active, intelligent and above all inquisitive animal with a strong inclination to explore and root about'. Yet this is the creature which is often denied any movement or activity and cruelly chained to the floor in intensive pig-rearing systems.

The pig-meat industry, one of the most strongly criticized areas of intensive farming, has been undergoing some welcome changes in recent years. A number of factors have been responsible. Government subsidies for farm buildings, by which taxpayers' money was used to encourage and support intensive methods of 'farming', have now been withdrawn. This makes outdoor rearing systems, requiring less capital outlay, economically attractive to producers. Wide-scale media publicity about the cruelties in intensive pig-meat production and the advent of the 'green consumer' have worried the industry. Powerful meat retailers, aware that intensive methods produce pork and bacon of inferior taste and texture, have been pressing for better quality.

However, it would be a great mistake to think that all the pork and bacon on sale today comes from less cruelly kept pigs. Far from it! About 30 per cent of it is imported from Holland and Denmark, where the production systems are highly intensive. In Britain, the vast majority of pigs fattened up for pork and bacon are still kept indoors, many of them in sterile conditions, and more than half of the breeding sows still endure close-confinement systems. Legal steps to outlaw these systems are unlikely, but pig-meat from kinder systems is now more easily available, putting it within the power of the caring consumer to put a stop to the abuses.

Close-confinement Systems

The worst cruelties in the pig industry involve many of our national population of about three quarters of a million breeding sows. These animals are kept to produce the litters of piglets which will be slaughtered at four to six months of age for bacon, pork, etc.

The breeding sows are kept for about two years, after which their most profitable breeding days are past (litters tend to become smaller) and they are slaughtered mainly for German sausages and other products which do not require the best-quality meat. For much of their productive lives they are half-starved, being fed less than half the calories their appetite requires. Otherwise, having been bred for such fast growth, they would become too fat to breed. Scientific tests have shown they are even hungry immediately after their daily feed. They will be fed more generously during late pregnancy and lactation.

The breeding sow is pregnant for most of her adult life. She is expected to produce five litters in just over two years and her pregnancies last for about four months. Usually, she is re-mated four or five weeks after giving birth.

Sows in close-confinement systems are kept, throughout their pregnancies, in individual metal-barred stalls which are so small that they are unable to take more than one step forward or one step backwards. Some are kept permanently tightly chained to the bars of the stall.

Bedding is not normally provided in these stalls and the sows stand and lie on a hard floor of concrete or metal slats. A heavy, hairless animal such as a pig has just as great a need for soft bedding as a human, and the deprivation is particularly acute in the case of pregnant creatures. Many of the sows suffer painful arthritic and rheumatoid conditions and also lameness, due to their chronic discomfort. Skin abrasions are common, particularly from the body tethers attached to those which are chained. Having nothing at all to occupy them, the sows resort to either biting their tether chain or stall bars, or to some other form of stereotyped behaviour. Sometimes they simply stand and chew for long periods with nothing but saliva in their mouths.

Dr G. M. Cronin studied the behaviour of nine sows, when they were first tethered in a close-confinement system, in 1985. In the paper he consequently published he gave this account of their first reaction to confinement:

> Following a brief and gentle tug on the tether chain, the sows threw themselves violently backwards, straining against the tether ... Sows thrashed their heads about as they twisted and turned in their struggle to free themselves. Often loud screams were emitted and occasionally individuals crashed bodily against the side bars of the tether stall. This sometimes resulted in the sows collapsing to the floor.

Dr Cronin reported that the sows he observed spent, on average, forty-five minutes in this panicked reaction before quietening down. Throughout the first two weeks of confinement they were seen occasionally either pulling at their tethers or aggressively biting at the stall bars, which suggested that the motivation to escape had not yet disappeared. Later behaviour, reported in this and other studies, suggests that the pigs eventually sink into inactivity, interspersed with the performance of stereotyped behaviour.

When independent scientists at the government-supported Scottish Farm Buildings Investigations Unit (now the Centre for Rural Building) were asked, in

1986, to review all available scientific evidence on the subject, they reached the following conclusions:

(1)   The close confinement of sows causes severe distress;

(2)   Sows adapt to close confinement, but the way in which they adapt resembles, in many respects, the development in humans of chronic psychiatric disorders.

When the sow is ready to give birth she is moved into another equally harsh and restricted environment. This is a metal cage-like structure known as a farrowing crate. It is designed to prevent her from crushing her piglets, a problem which arises mainly because her legs are so weak from lack of exercise that she tends to flop down on to the floor. Piglet-crushing is not a problem, only an occasional accident, when sows are kept free-range. In a natural environment a pig would build herself a nest, but in the farrowing crate she is often denied any straw and gives birth on a concrete or metal-grid floor. For the next three to four weeks, until the piglets are weaned and removed, she is kept in the farrowing crate, unable to move apart from standing up and lying down on her side to feed the piglets. About a week later the sow is mated again and starts another pregnancy.

The Ministry of Agriculture, which has been largely responsible for promoting, supporting and subsidizing intensive methods of animal rearing since the 1950s, appears to find it difficult to continue to justify the close-confinement pig systems. Their current Welfare Code for Pigs states that, 'the keeping of sows and gilts [a young, unbred sow] in stalls with or without tethers raises serious welfare problems'. It also strongly recommends the use of alternative systems in which 'animals' behavioural and exercise needs can be more fully met . . .'

Only the National Farmers' Union, ignoring all evidence, stoutly reassure the public (in their leaflet, *Looking After Pigs: Some Facts and Figures*) that:

> *Existing scientific knowledge is unclear on the extent to which pigs actually* need [*their emphasis*] *space, or whether close confinement causes distress.*

They conclude the same educational leaflet with the categorical assurance that:

> *Successful pig production is never – and can never be – achieved at the expense of animal welfare.*

In this respect, at least, they *are* correct. The poor quality of the pork which many of their members have been producing in these intensive systems has now been directly linked to the stress suffered by the pigs. Which is one of the reasons why quality conscious retailers like Marks & Spencer are now insisting on free-range sows and pigs fattened in better welfare systems.

Better Systems for Sows

Growing public concern over farm-animal welfare has led, in recent years, to the development of more humane indoor systems for housing breeding sows. Nearly 50 per cent of the breeding population is now either free-range (15 per cent) or group-housed in a variety of indoor systems which at least allow the animals the freedom to move around, the companionship of their own kind and straw or other bedding material to lie on and root in. Electronic feeding systems are often used to dispense food.

Critics point to aggressive behaviour as the one drawback. Sows have a tendency to fight, largely because factory farmers keep them in overcrowded conditions and in a state of hunger for much of the time. Feeding and other arrangements which help to eliminate aggression are, however, being developed. One such system automatically dispenses predetermined amounts of food on to the straw bedding, thus occupying the pig and satisfying its natural desire to root for its food. Given a sufficient outlet for normal activities, adequate space, comfortable conditions and good stockmanship, a group will quickly establish a 'pecking order' which largely eliminates conflict. As one experienced pigman put it: 'It's a poor farmer who has to chain his pigs to the ground in order to keep them unharmed!'

Fattening Pigs

The offspring of the breeding sows, which will be fattened up for four to six months to supply the bulk of the pork, ham and bacon in the shops, are raised by different systems from their mothers. Nearly all are kept in groups, usually of about thirty. The vast majority are reared indoors. This applies, during the winter, even on organic farms. However, the conditions in which they live vary a great deal.

At many factory farms, fattening houses are barren, dimly lit and windowless places where the piglets live on hard slatted or metal-mesh floors with no straw for comfort, bedding or play. With no outlet for activity or play they often become aggressive and injure each other. Tail biting is common, even cannibalism may occur. The factory farmers' answer to this is to cut off their tails. The ends of their incisor teeth are also cut off, partly for this reason and partly to protect the teats of the sow, now that she has been bred to give birth so frequently to large litters.

According to a leading expert, Professor Ingmar Eckesbo:

> *Tail-biting and cannibalism do not occur in pigs under normal conditions but result from the pig being understimulated in a barren environment with no bedding or from overstimulation owing to overcrowding and a high noise level.*

Some male piglets, usually those which will be reared for bacon, are subjected to the pain of castration without anaesthetic and without the operation being performed by a vet. This cruelty is performed to satisfy certain retailers and wholesalers who believe that boar meat becomes tainted with an unattractive flavour. In fact, piglets are killed at such an early age these days that the problem of flavour rarely arises.

Some producers, aware of public outrage which is turning the consumer against their product, are starting to introduce better conditions for fattening piglets. They find that the cost of bedding materials, extra space or reduced stocking density can be offset by bonuses from improved health, growth rate and feed conversion, and reduced stress, fighting and injury. Organic and free-range pig farmers often provide indoor housed piglets with rooting areas, rubbing posts and playthings like swinging rubber tyres, and find that this provides a better solution to aggression than the mutilations practised by the factory farmers.

Like most animals killed in slaughterhouses, pigs endure great stress and suffering from the time of their removal from the factories or farms where they have been reared to their eventual death. They seem particularly prone to terror and panic. Even *Farmers Weekly* writes of 'the chasing around and scrum seen on some units', as terrified, screaming animals are captured to be loaded on to lorries. In lorries and lairage at the slaughterhouse, and as they are finally driven to their slaughter, usually with the liberal use of electric goads, there is a great tendency for them to crowd together and clamber over their fellows, often injuring each other. Stunning procedures are far from foolproof, and slaughterhouses are inadequately inspected. At most, a low priority is given to animal welfare.

PLAICE

Plaice, along with many other flat fish, have the potential to live to a considerable age. A Ministry of Agriculture expert recently caught one aged forty-two! Those served up on the fish counter will usually have taken at least two or three years to reach minimum legal landing size, and the bulk of them will have lived for about five years, free in the sea. Particularly large plaice may even be teenagers.

They are caught by trawling nets, in their habitat at the bottom of the sea. Most are landed live on deck, and often meet a quick but nasty end when they are gutted immediately.

PRAWNS

Served in four out of every five restaurants, sold in a vast variety of convenience meals, prawns are now Britain's favourite seafood. Their popularity extends worldwide. As many as sixty countries fish or farm as many different species, and most of those we eat are imported. Some species are more correctly called 'shrimps', but tend to be known to the public as 'prawns'.

Without being a considerable expert, it would be extremely difficult to know the life history of those prawns which end up in your curry or cocktail. The best quality prawns, often sold shell-on, are caught in cold Arctic waters. Many others are fished out of warm seas in the Far East, or off the coast of South America. And you might well be eating farmed prawns.

Prawn farming thrives in Asia. Many of these farms trap young prawns, newly emerged from their larval stage in the sea, and fatten them up in ponds. Now a new industry is emerging which hatches and grows the prawns from eggs. There are more than fifteen hundred hatcheries in Taiwan alone.

At present, however, most of the world's prawns are still fished from the sea, in vast quantities, and meet their ends by a diversity of methods. Some are boiled alive in sea water, some are immersed in cold brine and frozen, others are air-blast frozen.

Can a prawn suffer pain? There is no reason to think not. Crustacea do have nervous systems, though less sophisticated than those of fish, and respond to noxious stimuli. There has been little research in this area, but all experts are agreed that a small creature, like a prawn, will die much more quickly than a large creature, like a lobster, when subjected to a change in body temperature. Prawns are thought to die 'near instantaneously' or 'in a few seconds' in boiling water. Death by freezing may take longer, but could be less cruel. Researchers find that temperatures below normal slow down the systems and movements of sea creatures, and could induce a state of torpor.

QUAILS

Raised in cages, fed on concentrates, often crowded together in hundreds or thousands in gloomy sheds, most of today's quails endure as wretched an existence as factory-farmed chickens. It is many years since these small migratory birds were shot as game in Britain. Some wild quail can still be found here in summer, but they have been protected by law since the 1950s, when their numbers were found to be seriously depleted. What you are nearly always getting, these days, when you order roast quail, is a bird raised in a very similar way to broiler chicken. And most of those pretty little spotted eggs are laid by quails kept in rows of small cages like battery hens.

The quail business is very much a microcosm of the poultry industry. Most oven-ready birds and eggs are supplied by a small number of specialist quail 'farms', using highly intensive methods. The fact that the quail farm might stock ten thousand birds or less, compared to the hundreds of thousands in a broiler- or battery-hen factory, makes little difference to the life of the bird itself.

No creature is able to adapt happily to modern intensive rearing methods, and these lively, flighty, semi-wild birds are particularly ill-suited to such conditions. The caged layers are prone to injuring themselves on the roofs of their cages as they try to fly. Fighting, feather-pecking and even cannibalism are rife among the birds caged together in hundreds and fattened up in eight weeks for the table.

Some smallholders keep smaller numbers of quail in kinder conditions with plenty of space and outdoor runs. Their eggs, or the table-birds for roasting, may be sold from the premises or local shops. But there is no statutory labelling of 'free-range', etc., for quail products and see-for-yourself is the best policy. Producers with nothing to hide are rarely reluctant to let a potential customer take a peep. But small does not always mean beautiful in the bird business, and behind the doors of even small sheds in pleasant rural locations lie some distressing sights – bare-backed birds under constant attack, air thick with dirt and dust, the little grey-brown bodies of those which failed to survive such conditions for even eight weeks littered around like forgotten floorcloths.

The ugliness of this business is often in sharp contrast to the image conveyed by those charming boxes of tiny speckled eggs displayed in the shops.

RABBIT

The rabbit, in its natural habitat, is a sensitive, social and most of all an *active* creature. It moves frequently, to explore, nibble, play and may cover several miles in a day. Reared in captivity, to produce meat, it spends its entire life huddled in a wire cage measuring about 2 × 3 ft.

In contrast to the huge poultry factories, housing as many as 100,000 birds, rabbit rearing in Britain is very small-scale. Much of the meat is produced by 'the little man' in garages, sheds, any type of cheap or abandoned building. But these mini-factory farms provide just as wretched a life for the poor confined creatures.

The typical rabbit farmer would be a retired trades-man, looking for a money-making hobby. Or, often, a young would-be entrepreneur who failed to make the promised fortune from selling water-filters or double-glazing, and is now duly impressed by the hard-sell tactics of the big men in the rabbit business. These are the companies who make their profits from selling rabbit-farming equipment and supplies.

'Rabbits are MONEY' (their capitals) booms the sales literature of one such company, in the north of

England. 'You grow rabbits to earn money – as a profitable animal they can outstrip most other animals.'

'Rabbits make money – that's why WE keep them,' they go on to explain, in case you've missed the message. 'You'll enjoy working with rabbits – no noise – no stink – no dust. Just quiet furry animals quietly making money . . .'

Indeed, from their sales literature (price £5), you can see that, for companies like this, rabbits certainly are MONEY. Want to learn how to rabbit farm? Then you need their *One Day Special Intensive Practical Tutorial on Profitable Rabbit Keeping* – price £45. Ready to set up? Then they will supply the breeding does, males and equipment at prices that soon tot up to thousands of pounds for any appreciable numbers. Then, of course, you may well need their marketing service, £45 to enrol and £25 a year, and so on, and so on . . .

To recoup this investment, the rabbit farmer expects a great deal from his breeding does. Most are mated at eighteen weeks and produce their first litter a month later. There is no 'heat' period in the female rabbit; she will ovulate at any time in direct response to the buck. Usually she will be re-mated about twenty days after giving birth, but some rabbit keepers re-mate them as quickly as three days afterwards. This way the doe can be made to undertake a double work load, feeding one litter as she gestates another.

The snag is that she may well be worn out, even before the eighteen months to two years working life normally expected of a breeding doe.

A nest-box, with bedding material, is introduced into the doe's cage when she is ready to give birth. It remains there only during the four weeks her offspring stay with her. For the remainder of the time she relies for her comfort only on a wire floor. This often results in sore hocks and secondary infections which extend to her joints. Rabbit 'processors' complain of the number of animals sent to them with sore feet and abscesses, causing health risks at the slaughterhouses.

Diarrhoea, ear infections and reproductive diseases are other all-too-common problems, which is why some vets recommend a rigorous culling policy. Explains J. Cowie-Whitney, PhD, MRCVS:

> Culling is a continuous process which occurs throughout all stages of the growing period. The rabbit may be culled because of disease, being surplus to requirements, physical injury, etc.

Rabbit farmers become adept at killing, holding the animal by the hind legs and breaking its neck with a quick twist. As the British Commercial Rabbit Association points out: 'Treatment of individual animals is seldom economic.'

The young rabbits are usually allowed to live for ten weeks before being killed, skinned, portion-packed and chilled for the shops and supermarkets. They are taken from their mothers after a month, and caged together for the remaining weeks until large enough to be sent live to the rabbit-processing plants. The collection and transport of rabbits leaves much to be desired. Collected by lorry at a centre point, they may travel around the countryside for up to twenty-four hours before reaching the slaughter-house. Usually they will be electrically stunned before being killed.

Only the fresh and chilled meat in the shops comes from the British rabbit business. Much of the frozen rabbit on sale, which is usually diced and darker in colour, is imported from China, where peasants usually keep them in colonies surrounded by close bamboo

fencing. Whether the Chinese rabbit lives a better life than his captive British counterpart is hard to say. It could hardly be worse.

SALMON

Ninety-seven per cent of the fresh salmon sold and served in Britain today is the product of the salmon-farming industry, which was established, in its present form, about twenty-five years ago, and has undergone a huge expansion during the past decade. Wherever your salmon is sold or served – fishmonger, supermarket or restaurant – assume it is farmed unless specifically labelled as 'wild' salmon.

The very speed at which salmon farming has grown has caused alarm among environmentalists. They fear that long-term consequences may have been overlooked (as they have been in other areas of intensive farming). Critics complain of the sewage-type pollution from faeces and food caused by keeping as many as a hundred thousand fish in a relatively small area of water, and the potentially hazardous chemicals used to control diseases and infestations. The wholesale shooting of seals, and other predators attracted to the salmon cages is another problem, as is the detrimental visual effect of the fish farms to areas of outstanding natural beauty. Many are situated in the sea lochs of Scotland.

But is salmon farming cruel to salmon? Even for animal-welfare organizations this is a difficult problem to answer, and attitudes among them vary from unease and concern to 100 per cent opposition. Science, as usual, has few answers. Little research has been done into the welfare of intensively farmed fish or animals, but experts agree that fish are capable of suffering stress as well as pain. They have stress hormones, similar to our own, which are elevated in response to stressful situations. So far, experiments designed to compare the level of those hormones in farmed and wild salmon (by Dr E. Donaldson of the Canadian Fisheries and Ocean Laboratories, Vancouver) have revealed little difference. But welfarists worry about the unnatural overcrowding of the farmed salmon in their cages and the suppression of powerful natural instincts.

Certainly salmon do not suffer the near-total restriction on movement endured by many intensively farmed animals, barely able to move at all. Although kept together in large numbers and in very restricted areas, they do at least have sufficient space to allow them to swim, albeit in dense shoals which are unnatural to their species.

Wild salmon start life in river gravel, and grow in the river from one to two years, when they start to undergo a major change in appearance and head down the rivers for the sea. Farmed salmon, which are bred from eggs stripped from breeding females at land-based hatcheries, and reared in tanks, or pens in freshwater lochs, undergo the same physical changes at about a year. At this stage they must be moved to salt water in order to survive. They are rushed there in tanks in lorries, boats and even helicopters.

For the next two years of their lives (most are killed at

around three years of age), the farmed salmon will live in underwater cages in tidal lochs or estuaries. Space and density will vary from farm to farm, but a typical steel cage would be 16 m (17½ yd) square and contain about ten thousand fish. A fish farm might consist of about ten such cages – a hundred thousand fish.

Despite their limited space, the fish swim a great deal and one observer has estimated that, swimming round and round in their cages, they distance as much as ten miles in a day. They often leap out of the water. While supporters of salmon-farming point out that this is part of the natural behaviour of salmon, critics fear that this is an expression of their constant state of frustration and liken their state to that of wild salmon whose migration upstream is thwarted by a fish dam.

The fish are fed on proprietary brands of pellets consisting largely of fishmeal. As with battery-produced eggs, which owe the yellowness of their yolks to a chemical colouring agent, the fish are fed a chemical 'pinking agent' in order to tint their flesh to the colour of that of wild salmon.

Farmed fish are killed in a variety of ways. The most commonly practised method is to stun the fish with one or two blows to the head using a club or 'priest'. In Shetland, salmon are often bled to death without prior stunning. Some salmon farmers stun the fish, prior to bleeding, by placing them in tanks with carbon dioxide bubbling through, but the fish go through a two-minute phase of 'frenzy' prior to loss of consciousness when this method is used.

SALMON (Canned)

Now that nearly all fresh salmon served in Britain is farmed fish, the most likely place to find wild salmon is in a can. The vast majority of canned salmon sold in

British shops is Pacific salmon imported from the USA and Canada. There it is still so profuse that it is less expensive to the British fish canner than the Atlantic salmon farmed in our waters.

As fish farming expands, the price-gap is narrowing. It may well be that, before long, farmed salmon will gain the price advantage and start filling the cans. Meanwhile, if you are opposed to fish farming, take comfort from the fact that the canned salmon will have enjoyed about three years in its natural habitat before being netted.

SARDINES (and PILCHARDS)

Sardines swim in large shoals in warm seas, and most of those we eat are netted, mainly by traditional methods, off the coasts of Morocco and Portugal. Those which survive suffocation crowded together in vast numbers in the nets expire quickly on board.

Pilchards are simply 'grown-up' sardines. Same fish, but grown older and bigger. The sardine will have been caught in its first year or two of life; the pilchard will have lived free for from two to six years.

The fresh sardines on sale here since the British acquired a taste for them on their Mediterranean holidays are really pilchards. But, if they are labelled 'pilchards', nobody buys them. If they are labelled 'sardines', they do. So they are always labelled 'sardines'.

SCALLOPS

Although the Japanese farm scallops, suspending them in bags in the sea, ours continue to enjoy a natural lifestyle. Scallops sold in Britain will usually have lived three to five years half-buried in the sand and gravel on the seabed. If left undisturbed they would live for as long as twenty years.

Most scallops are gathered by dredging the sea bottom,

although some are taken as a by-catch in white-fish trawling.

Scallops do not have the same ability as mussels and oysters to close their shells tightly and stay alive for long periods out of water. They can survive for two or three days in cold weather, but only about a day in warmer weather, unless kept in sea water. In this country they are rarely sold live.

Most catches of scallops will be taken to processing plants and will be killed as part of a process called 'shucking'. A knife is used to open the shell and remove the viscera. Usually this is done by hand, but where machines are used the live scallop may be first dropped in boiling water or steamed to open the shell.

SCAMPI

The ubiquitous 'scampi', now as common a feature of the British pub as beer, is a creature called the Norway lobster – or sometimes the Dublin Bay prawn. In size it measures midway between lobster and prawn, around four inches.

The Norway lobster lives free in the sea around our coasts and is captured in large quantities, mainly off Scotland. Most are caught in a specially designed light trawl, others are netted along with other fish, and some of the larger specimens are trapped in pots, like lobsters.

Although the French suck out the contents of the heads with great gusto, only the tail of the Norway lobster is consumed in this country. This, along with its tendency to discolour rapidly and to develop off-flavours if left intact, dictates a different fate to that of most captured crustacea. The head and shell are usually twisted off by hand, on deck, leaving only the tails to be landed.

SHARK

You've read the book, seen the film, and now you can eat the steak. Shark can now often be found on fish counters and is offered on restaurant menus. For today's many demi-vegetarians the firm texture of the fish makes it a good substitute for beefsteak.

Is it a kinder buy? Yes, in terms of the free life the fish has led, in the sea. Most are caught by baited hook and line, one of the less environmentally damaging of today's fishing methods, but some will have become entangled in the Pacific driftnets, notorious for their indiscriminate slaughter. Few fish meet a humane end, and the largest fish are the hardest to kill. When the shark is pulled on board it is 'stunned by a blow on the head', or 'bludgeoned', depending, no doubt, on expertise and the pro- or anti-fishing sympathies of the informant. After that, like the farm animals, it is bled to death.

SHEEP

Through a happy accident of nature, sheep have proved singularly resistant to the so-called progress of post-war agriculture, and lamb provides one of the kinder choices in comparison to other farmed meat.

The average lamb is allowed only a short life of around sixteen weeks. Born in spring, it is usually slaughtered by early autumn. But the chances are that it grew up with its own mother, played with other lambs, felt the sun on its back and lived in the hills or fields with the flock, in the old traditional way. Rare luxuries in these days of factory farming.

Sheep can obtain nearly all their nourishment from the short, rough grass which grows on the unfertile, hilly areas which make up about a third of the agricultural land of Britain. Land which has no other productive use. To this they owe their freedom.

Many British sheep are kept, or at least born and initially reared, in these upland areas. They are such efficient grazers of poorer pastures that even in the lowlands it generally costs less to keep them outdoors than feed them indoors. These days, lowland farmers often bring their breeding ewes into fully or partially enclosed buildings from December until after lambing in early spring, to prevent lambing losses and allow heavily grazed pasture to rest. Protection from the harshest of winter weather and better supervision during lambing compensates the sheep for this temporary curtailment of freedom. About 15 per cent of the lambs born outdoors, among the free-range flocks of the Scottish hills, die as babies from a combination of cold and malnutrition and the dying process can take many hours.

Sheep have, so far, benefited from their resistance to the scientists' attempts to manipulate their breeding pattern, although there are worrying signs that such practices, designed to make them more prolific, are creeping into sheep farming. They are seasonal breeders, mating only during late summer and autumn months, and giving birth just once a year. Artificial insemination, practised on many other farm animals, has so far proved too costly and complicated for general use on sheep.

Premature weaning does not, as in the case of pigs, bring the sheep back into season more quickly, and, generally, the most cost-efficient way of feeding lambs is to allow them to feed from their mothers. Hence the happy sight, so rare in modern farming, of mother and young in the fields together.

There is a small business in indoor intensive lamb rearing to produce 'new season's lamb' early in the year. But this accounts for only about 7 per cent of the industry at present.

Footrot, a very painful problem for sheep, is far too

common in many flocks, where up to 30 per cent of the animals may be lame at any one time. Some farmers simply accept this as a 'normal' state of affairs. One of the reasons is that a shepherd is now often expected to look after two to three thousand animals, instead of two to three hundred.

Sadly, the procedures by which sheep and lambs are killed are punctuated by the usual catalogue of unnecessary cruelties. Most are first subjected to the stress of auction markets, where the rough handling they often receive is even admitted by meat traders: 'We have found that lambs bought from auctions have twice the level of bruising of that from the deadweight suppliers,' meat wholesaler and abattoir owner David Maunder complained in *Farmers Weekly* (1 December 1989). 'For the integrity of the product this must be stopped, not only for appearance reasons, but also on welfare grounds.'

Handling sheep is difficult, because there is nothing much to 'hold on to'. Picking them up by the fleece causes them extreme pain, and can result in extensive bruising. Typical of the callous attitude shown to sheep, at markets, is the cruel practice of 'live grading', by which a large hole is punched in the ear of each animal. This unnecessary cause of pain could easily be avoided.

At best, auction selling means that sheep are twice exposed to loading, unloading, transport, handling and stress, prior to death. The practice has been encouraged by government subsidies (now being phased out as part of EEC policy) which have tended to give a modest financial advantage to sheep farmers who sold lambs via the auctions.

The electric stunning method, used on sheep prior to slaughter, is notoriously prone to error. Many lambs recover consciousness before being bled to death, which can take as long as five minutes, due to the method used for 'sticking' sheep which often fails to sever both main arteries. Surer methods of stunning are available, but profit motives prevail and animal welfare takes a low priority in most slaughterhouses. Mutton is a popular meat among Muslim communities. Sheep slaughtered for this market, and for orthodox Jews, are killed by being bled to death without being stunned.

Britain is the main producer of lamb in Europe and the growing practice of live exports is bringing notoriety to the industry. The horrific animal suffering involved has been the subject of exposés in the *Sunday Times*, *Observer*, *Daily Mirror* and many other newspapers. Lambs can be subjected to journeys as long as two or three days. What laws there are to ensure that they are fed, watered, rested and protected from overcrowding and injury are clearly unenforceable and widely flouted. Although this is not officially sanctioned, some English lambs even end up being slaughtered by the barbaric methods practised in many Spanish slaughterhouses.

We continue to import some of our own lamb from New Zealand, where a very extensive method of rearing is practised and the sheep and lambs are largely left to fend for themselves. But the vast bulk of lamb sold in Britain today is British reared.

SHRIMP

Unlike prawns, which are mainly imported, the brown shrimp is British. It tends to live close to shore and is often abundant in estuaries. Most are trawled, either by boat or tractor at low tide, from the Wash, the Thames Estuary, the Solway Firth and, of course, Morecambe Bay.

Technically, many of the prawns we eat are more correctly known as shrimps, but this small brownish crustacean, laboriously prised from its shell by the patient

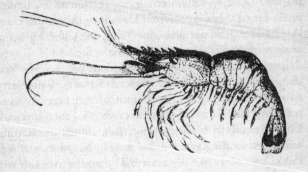

seaside holiday-maker, is most commonly known as such. One shrimp provides precisely one calorie. Multiply this by vast numbers if you pot it in lashings of butter.

Like most crustacea the shrimp is killed/cooked in boiling water. Its very small size should ensure it a quick death.

SKATE (and RAY)

Most of the fish sold as 'skate' are actually 'ray', but both are members of the same distinctively shaped wide-winged family. Skate are becoming scarce, and it is likely that ray will diminish in the same way. They are much less prolific than most other fish, and so less able to withstand the intensity of modern fishing. While a cod may lay a million eggs, and a plaice up to half a million, the ray family members only produce about fifty to a hundred and fifty eggs each year. The capsules in which the eggs are laid – dark green semi-translucent cases with 'horns' at each end – are often washed up on shore, and are known as 'mermaid's purses'.

Skate spend most of their time lying at the bottom of the sea, only occasionally moving up in the water. If left undisturbed they may well live for as long as thirty or forty years and reach enormous sizes, with wing spans as wide as six to eight feet. However, because of their wide-winged shape, even young skate, which have not yet reached maturity and reproduced themselves, are particularly vulnerable to being captured in the netting in sea-bottom trawling, which is another problem affecting their survival. They are usually landed live on deck. Those below legal minimum landing size will be thrown back into the sea, but not all of them will survive. The marketable fish will usually have lived in the sea for three or more years. On deck they will be gutted, shortly after being caught.

In some fishing areas, like Lowestoft, skate are still caught by the more traditional and environmentally friendly method of baited lines, but the labour involved in baiting the many hooks on commercial fishing lines have led to a decrease in popularity of this method. These days the majority are captured by trawling.

SNAILS

You might feel it shouldn't even happen to a snail, but happen it has. He/she (they are hermaphrodite) has been brought indoors, crowded together with other snails in a sterile environment, fed on concentrates, had its natural behaviour pattern changed by artificial tempera-ture, been selected for fast-feeding and fast-growth . . .

In short, the snails – or, at least, some of the snails – are now being factory-farmed in Britain. They are kept in polypropylene trays, which measure 4 × 2 ft and each house as many as five thousand young snails or five hundred full-grown adults.

What the snail feels about this is anybody's guess. Certainly it is losing sleep about it, being dissuaded from its natural winter hibernation by artificially high snail-house temperatures. Britain's free-range snail farmers take a dim view of such methods. They have formed the British Snail Farmers' Association, dedicated to letting snails graze outdoors on natural greenery, in parks, pens or large-mesh tunnels.

Free-range snails grow at normal speed, hibernate in winter, and take about eighteen months to reach edible size. Factory farmers have speeded this up to just four months by rearing fast-growing and giant species by intensive methods.

All this pace and change stems from an expanding European market. Snail-hungry France imports large quantities of its *escargots*. In Britain some hard-selling middle-men, similar to the kind you find behind rabbit farming, are marketing know-how and equipment to those hoping to cash in by intensive snail farming. Punters pay for training courses, advisory services, food, equipment, and £5 a head for each 'point-of-lay' breeding snail.

Most snails are killed, like crustacea, in boiling water, and are thought to die quickly. Sometimes, however, restaurants immerse live snails in brine for 24–36 hours instead. During this slow death the lid of the brine container has to be weighted down to prevent them from climbing out.

Some of the canned snails sold in Britain are still imported from France and many, but not all, of these will have been gathered in the wild.

SOLE

The sole is a very fussy feeder and appears to live almost entirely on one specific type of seabed worm known as the bristleworm or ragworm. Its round muscular little mouth seems specifically made to suck them up, like spaghetti, from the seabed mud or sand.

Along with its fellow flatfish, the sole lives near the bottom of the sea. Most of those we eat are captured by trawlers in the English Channel and will have lived a minimum of two years, usually more. The bulk will be around five years old. They are usually landed live, and will be gutted on deck, immediately.

SQUID (Calamares)

Most Brits acquired their taste for it in Spain. But the fresh squid we are served at home is caught in our own coastal waters, where it occurs in large quantities. British fishermen tend to catch it by accident in netting and trawling other fish. In other seas, particularly near Japan, they go 'squid jigging' at night – flashing lights and jigging baited lines up and down to attract large shoals of this much-consumed cephalopod.

The squid is related to the octopus, but differs from its larger, wiser, more sedentary cousin in many ways. It darts about with great speed – faster even than fish. Another oddity is its extremely delicate skin, easily damaged, which makes it an unlikely future candidate for fish farming.

The squid grows at a phenomenal rate and lives a very short natural life of little more than two years. If caught, it dies very quickly out of water and is unlikely to survive more than a few minutes on deck. Squid are not normally gutted at sea; they are simply washed and packed in ice.

STURGEON

Caviare, as we all know, comes from the virgin sturgeon, and the virgin sturgeon is a very fussy fish. It will only thrive in the Caspian Sea, which is the sole source of all the caviare we can't afford to eat. Only the Russians and Iranians, who border the Caspian, can fish for sturgeon – and it wisely resists the utmost efforts of other countries to try to cultivate it.

The occasional sturgeon can be found elsewhere, even in the Thames where, once quite common, it is the legal property of the Queen. But these days, sturgeon outside the Caspian are exceedingly rare. Hence the price of caviare.

The Beluga is the king of sturgeons – the largest and most prized of the three kinds which are caught. Growing up to twelve feet in length, it takes about twenty years to mature and produce the eggs which are stripped from its dead body to fill the precious pots.

The two smaller types of sturgeon mature more quickly. Measuring from four to seven feet, they used not to be fished until they had reached about twelve years of age. Now greedy, over-speedy fishing methods are plundering the Caspian along with all the world's seas. There is talk of making the Beluga an endangered species.

Meanwhile, those sturgeon which remain at least enjoy a much longer life in the habitat of their own choice than most edible creatures.

TROUT

Unless you caught it yourself, you can safely assume that the trout on your plate comes from a fish farm. British native brown trout are not commercially viable and sea trout are only sold in a few areas, like the Yorkshire and East Anglian coasts. Trout in the shops and on the restaurant menu are nearly always farm-reared rainbow trout.

While most salmon farms are in Scotland, trout farms are widely spread all over Britain. Unlike most intensive farmers, trout farmers tend to practise glasnost and many, particularly the smaller ones, encourage the public to visit and look around.

Certainly, what you see there does not have the distressing impact of an intensive poultry or pig unit, although many of the usual ingredients of factory farming are present. Breeding patterns are manipulated, breeding fish (not their offspring) being treated with hormones to produce only females, which can be more speedily reared than males, have better flesh and tend to be less aggressive. Density is extremely high, particularly at the larger farms which often keep the fish in long, narrow concrete tanks, known as raceways. A typical raceway, 120 × 6 ft (3½ ft deep) can accommodate as many as 60,000 young sardine-sized trout, because of the high volume of oxygen-supplying fresh water constantly passing through. Availability of oxygen largely determines the number of fish which can be kept in an area of water.

With this high stocking density comes the usual high risk of disease, which has to be counteracted with chemicals, and potential problems with pollution.

However, from the welfare point of view, there is less evidence of obvious suffering. The trout, particularly those in ponds, do not appear to be in as alien an environment as, for instance, the wretched battery hen or rabbit in its cruelly comfortless wire cage. Overcrowding is not sufficiently bad to prevent movement (as in the case of the broiler chicken) and the fish – particularly when fed with pellets several times a day – dart about in a lively way. Cannibalism appears to be well controlled by the all-female selection and frequent 'grading'. Only fish of the same size are kept together in each pond or raceway.

The RSPCA, although confessing to 'unease' about fish farming, do not feel that sufficient is known, at the present time, for them to condemn the system on welfare grounds.

Most trout farms are near rivers, which they channel off to gain the constant flow of unpolluted water required. Usually, eggs are bought from hatcheries, and the tiny newly hatched fish are kept indoors at first, swimming round in large tanks in the farm's rearing unit until they are ready to be moved outside.

The trout takes about a year to reach market size, and fish-farm killing methods vary. Sometimes carbon dioxide is used in water for stunning, but a high proportion of trout are not stunned but left to die on crushed ice. Cooling them increases the time to loss of consciousness to over ten minutes.

Some trout farms permit the cruel practice of allowing punters to hook, play and return trout to the rearing pens, so that a fish may be captured several times prior to slaughter. Stress and any physical handling can cause chronic damage and clearly this practice causes a completely unnecessary increase in suffering.

Trout farms are very diverse in character. You might find a small local one which keeps fish in earth-bottomed ponds, a large one which uses concrete-lined raceways or galvanized circular tanks, or even one in a Scottish loch in which the trout are kept in floating cages. The British Trout Association will send a list of trout farms, all over Britain, many of which can be visited by those who wish to make up their own minds about trout farming. Write to them with a stamped addressed envelope at PO Box 2, Clitheroe, Lancashire BB7 3ED.

TUNA

In recent years, tuna fishing has been the target of campaigns by environmentalists in both America and

Britain. Concern has centred on two specific methods of tuna fishing.

Thanks to the efforts of Greenpeace, most people are aware of the notorious 'wall of death' fishing methods being practised by the environmentally unfriendly Japanese and the Taiwanese. Near-invisible plastic filament nets, measuring an average of twenty-five miles in length, are left floating in the oceans. Their main target, in the South Pacific, is a particularly valuable species of tuna, the albacore tuna, which has a creamy white flesh, much prized in tuna-hungry America. Hardly any albacore is sold in Britain, but it is thought that there is a considerable by-catch of skipjack (Britain's favourite tuna) in these nets.

Not only are these high-seas driftnets killing albacore at such a rate that there are fears of a population collapse, but hundreds of thousands of other sea creatures – dolphins, whales, seals, porpoises, turtles and many others – are being wastefully and pointlessly killed as they too become entangled in the nets.

Most tuna are caught in the Pacific, and the dolphins have also become the victims of a tuna-fishing method practised in certain specific areas (including the eastern tropical Pacific) where dolphins and a species of tuna called yellowfin have a particularly close association. A school of dolphins, easily detectable near the surface of the water, signals to the fishing fleets that a shoal of tuna may be swimming underneath. The method used to capture them is to surround both tuna and dolphins with a circular net which is then drawn in tightly. Being air-breathing marine mammals, the dolphins are drowned. Until methods were introduced to curtail this slaughter, it is estimated that as many as six million dolphins were killed in this way, and that around a hundred thousand are still killed annually. However, hardly any of the tuna caught in this part of the world is imported into Britain.

Where the issue becomes complex, for British buyers of tuna, is that tuna caught by the fishing fleets of one country is often frozen for export to another country for canning. Much British-bought canned tuna comes from Thailand, for instance, a major canning country which gets its tuna from many sources, not all environmentally friendly.

What about cruelty to the tuna itself? Like most of the fish we eat, the tuna has a completely free and natural life in the sea and suffers the usual brutal death involved in fishing methods. The vast majority of canned tuna sold in Britain is skipjack tuna. The fishing method most commonly used for skipjack, which is one of the smaller species of tuna, is purse seining – which is not usually associated with dolphin killing, other than in certain specific areas such as the eastern tropical Pacific. Most fish which swim in large shoals – salmon, pilchards, mackerel and herring, as well as many types of tuna – are caught in this way. The tuna will be encircled with a net which is then drawn in tightly around them until the fish are a solid, flapping, milling mass alongside the vessel. Then a scoop net is dipped into the mass of fish and swung inboard to the hold. Clearly, many of the tuna will suffer injury as part of this procedure.

On board, tuna are not gutted, like many other fish. Because they swim in warm seas, under tropical conditions, the emphasis is on freezing them with great speed. They are immediately placed in cargo wells filled with sea water at freezing point which extracts their body heat rapidly. Most of those which survive the netting will die of cold. Little research has been done into humane methods of killing fish, but there are indications that rapid lowering of body temperature may be less cruel than the rapid raising of temperature, as in the case of boiling shellfish.

Two other methods used to catch tuna are longline fishing – in which a line which may be several miles long and has many baited hooks is floated in the water – and pole and line from fishing boats which attract schools of tuna to them by throwing bait overboard. These methods, pole and line in particular, usually have the advantage of avoiding large-scale needless slaughter of other sea creatures.

TURBOT

Turbot is a large, luxury fish, which has attracted the attention of the fish farmers. Those on sale from May to October are mainly free-living fish from the sea. They will have been trawled or become entangled in the netting which is sometimes set in British waters to catch them. Turbot served up during winter months is sometimes farmed fish imported from Spain.

Turbot grow to marketing size in two to three years in warm seas, but take five years to reach the same size in our own colder waters. One British company farms them in the warm effluent water from Hunterston nuclear power station – but is now concerned only with exporting stock for overseas farms. The farmed turbot we eat has been reared in land-based tanks in the coastal areas of Spain and fed mainly on sand eels.

TURKEYS

Ninety per cent of British turkeys are factory-farmed, in intensive conditions. Behind those breast rolls, crispy crumb steaks and oven-ready birds lies another sad story of creatures bred and fed for unnatural growth and crowded together in cramped and sterile conditions.

Most turkeys are reared behind firmly locked doors by a small number of major companies, which surround their activities with great secrecy. Turkey tycoons are anxious to show off their products, but certainly not their live birds. Even telephone inquiries are met with long silences and reluctance to give information or even reveal the names of the staff.

In fact, many turkeys are reared in a similar way to broiler chickens, crowded into purpose-built sheds in vast numbers. (Others are reared in close confinement in buildings known as 'pole barns', open sided, though netted in.) A single shed may hold as many as fifteen thousand birds. Each bird is allocated a little more space than a broiler chicken in relation to its size, but the turkey lives a longer life, of up to twenty-four weeks, which often means more prolonged suffering. Longevity is no bonus for factory-farmed poultry.

Turkeys are particularly active birds, more closely related to the pheasant than the chicken. Their nature makes them even more than usually ill-suited for a life of close confinement. Aggression is the inevitable result of the unnatural and stressful conditions in which they live, conditions which could easily be improved were the industry to show concern about the suffering of the birds. Instead, their answer to this problem is to cut off the end of the turkeys' beaks with a red-hot blade. This treatment, described as an 'essential aid to management' by the Ministry of Agriculture, has been scientifically proved to cause prolonged and possibly permanent pain when inflicted on chickens. It is unlikely to be less painful for turkeys. Despite beak trimming, intensively reared turkeys still tend to peck at each other relentlessly. Eye injuries can lead to the destruction of the eyeball and about 7 per cent of the birds die in their sheds.

Like chickens, turkeys have been bred to put on weight at a greater rate than their legs are comfortably able to support. Often, slipped tendons cause legs to collapse or become deformed, and arthritis and ulcerated feet are a common problem. Many turkeys carry their great weight only with considerable pain. They have been bred to such an unnatural weight and state that natural breeding is now impossible and artificial insemination is used on all breeding turkeys.

All factory-farmed creatures, crowded together in large numbers, are particularly prone to disease and the turkey is no exception. The widespread use of drugs is required to control outbreaks of diseases like turkey rhino-tracheitis, haemorrhagic enteritis and 'blackhead', which damages their livers.

Turkeys are slaughtered by a system so cruel that it has been described as 'diabolical' by a scientist who has studied it. The live birds are suspended upside-down, in shackles, on a conveyor belt and gradually moved towards an electrically charged container of water in which they will be stunned when their heads make contact. However, the speed of the overhead line is very slow, and this is a long drawn-out process. Before being stunned, many of the birds receive an electric shock from trailing wings, or splashes of water. Birds have been observed to suffer this acute pain for several seconds before being rendered unconscious.

British law allows the turkey producer to suspend the birds upside-down for as long as six minutes before they are stunned. Supporting such a great weight on its weak limbs 'must be agony for the bird', according to an experienced veterinary expert. A fact which appeared not to worry the British Turkey Federation, which encouraged the growth of giant birds with its annual competition for the heaviest turkey, conducted with much Christmas jollity. Aware of growing protests from animal welfarists, it finally let this tasteless stunt lapse in 1990.

VEAL CALVES

Before the Second World War, veal was the tender flesh

of very young calves – usually the unwanted offspring of the dairy herds, slaughtered at just a few days old.

The modern veal industry is concerned with growing such animals to a much greater size and weight, but without allowing their flesh to mature in the natural way. The aim is to produce almost full-grown animals with white, baby-tender flesh. The methods used to achieve this require abnormal feeding and constraint on exercise, and, in the case of much of the veal still consumed in Britain, a degree of cruelty which has become notorious – even in an age when extreme cruelty has become normal practice in the treatment of farm animals.

Commercially reared veal calves do not graze in fields.* Those who believe that the farm animal should at least be allowed this minimum basic freedom won't want to eat this unnatural and unnecessary meat. But for those who eat veal, or serve it in their restaurants, 'which veal?' has now become an important question in animal welfare.

Three types of veal are now sold or served in Britain. The methods by which they are produced differ greatly in terms of the cruelty involved. There is British veal, sold in some of the supermarkets – and produced by far the most humane method. This veal is decidedly pink in colour, but tastes no different from white veal. At the other end of the scale there is the white veal served in most restaurants. This is veal produced in the Dutch veal-crate system. The third type of veal, sold in some supermarkets, is from the Dutch 'group-housed' system, which presents just a modest improvement in welfare on the appalling cruelties of the crate.

The veal-crate system was banned in Britain in 1990. However, there was no ban on the calves of British dairy cows being exported to be reared in the Dutch crates,

* There is one small source of field-reared grey veal; details on pages 64–5.

and about 300,000 are estimated to be exported each year to suffer this fate. Common Market rules do not allow a ban on the import of crate-reared veal, and most of the veal served in British restaurants still comes from this source. New EEC legislation, now in the pipeline, bans only the very worst excesses of the system and does not come into effective force until the end of the century.

Here are the basic details of the three systems which produce veal served or sold in Britain today.

White 'Restaurant' Veal: the Crate System

This method of rearing calves for veal was developed by the Dutch shortly after the war. The near-white flesh of very young calves was much prized by many Europeans, but clearly a small animal, slaughtered after only a few days, will only supply a modest quantity of such meat.

Calves reared in a natural way start to nibble grass during the first week of life. This supplements their mother's milk with iron, the one mineral which the milk lacks and which is necessary for the healthy development of the calf. Once iron gets into its system the flesh of the calf will begin to turn pink, and gradually deepen to the colour of beef.

The only way to prevent this natural process of development is to incarcerate the animal so that it is unable to obtain the nutrient it craves so much that it will even suck a rusty nail. The way to keep its flesh baby-tender is to deprive it of any exercise. This the Dutch set out to do with a maximum of efficiency.

Calves, destined for the veal system, are taken from their mothers a day or two after birth. Those exported from Britain will be subjected to long harrowing journeys after suffering the fear and stress of the livestock markets. On arrival at the veal unit they will be confined in narrow crates or pens. Here they will stay until, often too weak to walk, they are dragged out for slaughter about five months later.

The crates are so small, usually 22 × 54 inches, that the calves are unable even to lie down in a comfortable position. They must hunch up on the hard slatted floor as best they can. Unable to turn around to lick and groom themselves, they can become coated with excrement and have no way of protecting themselves from flies. Their knee joints often become swollen from chronic discomfort.

Fed only milk, the calves will go to desperate lengths to satisfy their compelling urges to suck, ruminate on solid food and obtain iron. They will even chew through wood in their struggle to obtain roughage. Metal fitments, which would be sucked in the search for iron, have to be avoided in the crates.

Despite all these precautions, some of the calves still succeed in finding a tiny trace of the mineral they crave. Iron is present in their bodies at birth, and minute quantities are expelled in their own urine. Calves will desperately lick the traces of their urine from the slatted floors of their crates. This sometimes results in a pale pink tinge to the veal produced from a particular animal. Such veal is usually exported to Britain where we are less fussy about the whiteness of the meat than other Europeans.

The veal industry has thrived on the Common Market surplus of milk. The aim of the producers is to feed it into the calves as fast as possible, for conversion into flesh. To do this, they maintain a high temperature in the veal factory, and deny the thirsty animals water so that they are compelled to gulp down unnatural and discomforting quantities of milk.

Obviously it is difficult to keep these sick and suffering animals alive, even for five months. Heavy medication is used to control the chronic diarrhoea, pneumonia, septi-caemia and other ailments which are such a problem in the veal units. They are also kept in almost perpetual darkness to reduce movement and distressing mooing.

This is the method by which the veal served in the majority of British restaurants is produced.

Group-housed Dutch Calf Veal

One major Dutch veal company has initiated a slightly better system for calf rearing, and the meat produced is sold in some British stores. The calves are kept together in small groups. Herd animals have a strong need for the company of their own kind, and this at least spares them the stress of individual incarceration.

The feeding system for these calves also offers some improvements. Their milk diet is supplemented by a limited quantity of straw or other roughage. This pro-vides them with a little iron and some solids to satisfy their need to ruminate.

These animals are still not allowed bedding material, and stand and sleep on hard slats. The space in which they are confined, although allowing the calf the 'luxury' of being able to turn around and groom itself, is still exceedingly limited.

This is a step forward in European veal production, and welcome as such, but still hardly represents a humane way in which to rear animals.

British-reared Veal Calves

The British method of rearing veal calves is certainly very much kinder than that practised in other European countries. Even before the legislation banning the system, many British veal producers had bowed to public pres-sure and banned it themselves (after a vigorous campaign to alert the public by Compassion in World Farming).

An excellent illustration of the power that can be exerted by consumer boycotts.

While Dutch veal calves are reared in huge factories, in tens of thousands, most British calves are reared in a small-scale way in barns on mixed farms in the West Country. They are always housed in groups, usually of twenty to thirty animals.

Straw, or some other form of bedding material will be provided, but the quantity and the general comfort of the animals will vary from farm to farm. The animals are allowed some straw to eat but, on its own, this is not sufficient to stimulate normal rumen development. They still live largely on milk and, as a result, produce large quantities of near-liquid excrement which does not make it easy to keep them clean and comfortable.

The buildings, often existing farm buildings and not purpose-built, are usually comfortably cool, and the animals are normally provided with water for most, although not all, of their lives. Water is withheld during their first weeks, until they have learned to feed from the mechanical teats which supply their milk feed.

British veal producers take care to show inquiring journalists into buildings where only very young calves are housed. At that stage the space allowed them provides plenty of room for them to walk around. It will become considerably more cramped as they more than double in size, but, again, is a big improvement on the space allowed in the European veal factories, even for the group-housed calves.

All in all, the British veal calf lives a sad, sterile life compared to that of animals allowed to graze in fields. But it is less cruelly treated than some other factory-farmed creatures – most poultry and pigs kept in close confinement systems for instance – and spared much of the extreme suffering of the Dutch veal calf.

WHELKS

The world is worried about the sex life of the whelk! These carnivorous seabed snails are turning hermaphrodite, and from America, Asia, Australasia and the Mediterranean Sea come scientific sightings of whelk penises – on female whelks! Not surprisingly, with such an unappealing problem, they are failing to reproduce. Whelks are dying out in many parts of the world.

As always, the problem can be traced back to man and his nasty, poisonous pollution. In this case it is a highly toxic substance (TBT) used in the paint for boats' hulls to discourage algae, limpets and barnacles. This slowly diffuses into the water killing plants and causing death or dire problems to marine animals, a problem which the chemical companies clearly failed to envisage, along with so many others.

Britain has been among the first to place at least a partial ban on the use of this poison. Since 1987 it has been banned on boats less than 25 m long. As a result, we still have some whelks crawling around at the bottom of the sea and enjoying a normal sex life. They are caught, like crabs and lobsters, in baited pots.

Your seaside whelk will have lived a natural life, but possibly a short one compared to that of most other sea creatures we eat. Whelks do most of their growing, and reach edible size of about one inch in shell length, during their first year. Left alone they go on growing gradually and can become very large during their natural lifespan of ten years or more.

Usually, whelks are boiled in sea-water near the place of landing. They take eight to ten minutes to cook. If they are small, it is thought that a lethal body temperature will be reached in seconds.

WHITEBAIT

Fried whitebait, one of those first-course 'inevitables' of the average British restaurant, is a dish made up of infant fish, mainly young herring and sprats. A controlled amount of fishing is allowed in the nursery fishing grounds near Britain's coast to supply this particular dish, but we import most of our whitebait from Holland and Denmark. These countries catch vast quantities of undersized, immature fish (which have not yet reproduced to replenish their number) in order to feed their factory-farmed pigs. Just one example of the many ways in which the intensive farming of animals depletes rather than increases world food supplies.

WILD BOAR

Wild boar may be wild by nature, but not by lifestyle when it is offered on a British restaurant menu. Almost certainly it will be a product of one of those alternative enterprises which mushroom almost hourly in British farming. Boar still roam free in some parts of Europe, but are long gone from the forests here.

Wild-boar breeders keep their animals in a variety of ways. Some are allowed to root around in areas of fenced-off woodland. Others will be confined indoors in small pens. Unfortunately, their legal classification as 'dangerous wild animals', rather than 'game', detracts from their lifestyle. The costly fencing, required by law, leads to a tendency to keep them indoors (albeit in straw-bedded pens) or to confine them in small outdoor areas. It also means that they must be sent to the slaughterhouse, rather than shot on the farm. All pigs display obvious signs of terror during capture, transportation and waiting time at the slaughterhouses, and the traumas are thought to be even greater for such semi-wild animals as these.

Generally, wild boar are not as intensively farmed as many ordinary pigs but in no way enjoy the more natural life of game. Farmed in a small way, they escape the worst cruelties of some of the big pig factories, and have a more prolonged life. The piglet, which grows relatively slowly, won't be ready for slaughter for nearly a year. The breeding sow might well be kept for more than five years – about twice the lifespan of factory-farmed pig.

Wild-boar liver pâté, sometimes found on delicatessen counters, is usually imported from Belgium. Often the proportion of wild-boar liver is only 20 per cent; it is combined with ordinary pig's liver and other ingredients.

FOR THE BEST IN PAPERBACKS, LOOK FOR THE

In every corner of the world, on every subject under the sun, Penguin represents quality and variety – the very best in publishing today.

For complete information about books available from Penguin – including Puffins, Penguin Classics and Arkana – and how to order them, write to us at the appropriate address below. Please note that for copyright reasons the selection of books varies from country to country.

In the United Kingdom: Please write to *Dept E.P., Penguin Books Ltd, Harmondsworth, Middlesex, UB7 0DA.*

If you have any difficulty in obtaining a title, please send your order with the correct money, plus ten per cent for postage and packaging, to *PO Box No 11, West Drayton, Middlesex*

In the United States: Please write to *Dept BA, Penguin, 299 Murray Hill Parkway, East Rutherford, New Jersey 07073*

In Canada: Please write to *Penguin Books Canada Ltd, 2801 John Street, Markham, Ontario L3R 1B4*

In Australia: Please write to the *Marketing Department, Penguin Books Australia Ltd, P.O. Box 257, Ringwood, Victoria 3134*

In New Zealand: Please write to the *Marketing Department, Penguin Books (NZ) Ltd, Private Bag, Takapuna, Auckland 9*

In India: Please write to *Penguin Overseas Ltd, 706 Eros Apartments, 56 Nehru Place, New Delhi, 110019*

In the Netherlands: Please write to *Penguin Books Netherlands B.V., Postbus 195, NL–1380AD Weesp*

In West Germany: Please write to *Penguin Books Ltd, Friedrichstrasse 10–12, D–6000 Frankfurt/Main 1*

In Spain: Please write to *Alhambra Longman S.A., Fernandez de la Hoz 9, E–28010 Madrid*

In Italy: Please write to *Penguin Italia s.r.l., Via Como 4, I-20096 Pioltello (Milano)*

In France: Please write to *Penguin Books Ltd, 39 Rue de Montmorency, F-75003 Paris*

In Japan: Please write to *Longman Penguin Japan Co Ltd, Yamaguchi Building, 2–12–9 Kanda Jimbocho, Chiyoda-Ku, Tokyo 101*

FOR THE BEST IN PAPERBACKS, LOOK FOR THE 🐧

FOOD AND COOKING IN PENGUIN

The Fratelli Camisa Cookery Book   Elizabeth Camisa

From antipasti to zabaglione, from the origins of gorgonzola to the storage of salami, an indispensable guide to real Italian home cooking from Elizabeth Camisa of the famous Fratelli Camisa delicatessen in Soho's Berwick Street.

A Table in Tuscany   Leslie Forbes

With authentic recipes and beautiful illustrations, artist and cook Leslie Forbes evokes the rich flavour of Tuscany, from its Renaissance palaces to its robust red Chianti. More than a cookery book and more than mere travel writing, *A Table in Tuscany* is a culinary odyssey.

The Food and Cooking of Eastern Europe   Lesley Chamberlain

Diverse, appetizing and often surprisingly sophisticated, the cuisine of Eastern Europe goes far beyond the goulash and beetroot soup familiar to the West. From the refreshing fruit soups of Hungary to the fish dishes of Dalmatia, this is a fascinating tour of Eastern gastronomy.

Out to Lunch   Paul Levy

Gloriously entertaining essays from Britain's best-known writer on food and drink as he eats out around the world. Whether you want to know more about truffle-hunting, cheeses, aphrodisiacs or the great American sandwich, or whether people actually do eat dogs in Macao, all the answers are here.

The Penguin Book of Jams, Pickles and Chutneys   David and Rose Mabey

'An excellent book; practical, personal and suggestive, every recipe's clearly the result of real experience and written with great charm' – *The Times*

More Easy Cooking for One or Two   Louise Davies

This charming book, full of ideas and easy recipes, offers even the novice cook good wholesome food with the minimum of effort.

FOR THE BEST IN PAPERBACKS, LOOK FOR THE 🐧

FOOD AND COOKING IN PENGUIN

Traditional Jamaican Cookery Norma Benghiat

Reflecting Arawak, Spanish, African, Jewish, English, French, East Indian and Chinese influences, the exciting recipes in this definitive book range from the lavish eating of the old plantocracy to imaginative and ingenious slave and peasant dishes.

Cooking in a Bedsit Katharine Whitehorn

Practical and light-hearted, the perfect book for those cooking in limited space, with little time and less money – problems that can easily be surmounted with imagination, common sense and a great deal of newspaper. 'All parents with bedsitter children should send them a copy' – *Observer*

The Beginner's Cookery Book Betty Falk

Revised and updated, this book is for aspiring cooks of all ages who want to make appetizing and interesting meals without too much fuss. With an emphasis on healthy eating, this is the ideal starting point for would-be cooks.

Jane Grigson's Fruit Book

Fruit is colourful, refreshing and life-enhancing; this book shows how it can also be absolutely delicious in meringues or compotes, soups or pies.

Fast Food for Vegetarians Janette Marshall

Packed with ideas for healthy, delicious dishes from Caribbean vegetables to rose-water baklava, this stimulating book proves that fast food does not have to mean junk food.

Malaysian Cookery Rafi Fernandez

A step-by-step guide to the intoxicating, fragrant, colourful cuisine of Malaysia: the origins of its three distinct culinary strands, traditional cooking techniques and customs, where to buy the more exotic ingredients – and a mouthwatering selection of recipes.

FOR THE BEST IN PAPERBACKS, LOOK FOR THE 🐧

FOOD AND COOKING IN PENGUIN

The Philosopher in the Kitchen   Jean-Anthelme Brillat-Savarin

In this utterly unprecedented collection of recipes, experiences, reflections, history and philosophy, gastronomy is raised to the level of an art. Witty, shrewd and anecdotal, it contains both some superb recipes for food and some highly satisfying observations on life.

The Food and Cooking of Russia   Lesley Chamberlain

'The first really good book on this fascinating subject. I read it from cover to cover as one would a novel' – Paul Levy. 'A fine book ... recipes to suit all tastes and moods – from the refined traditions of the nineteenth-century nobility to Ukrainian peasant dishes and spicy creations from Central Asia' – Alan Davidson

Scottish Regional Recipes   Catherine Brown

Bridal cake from Orkney, chicken stovies from the Highlands, Morayshire apples from the north-east ... Born out of local conditions and shaped by ingenuity and care throughout the centuries, these robust and satisfying recipes have stood the test of time.

English Bread and Yeast Cookery   Elizabeth David

'Here is a real book, written with authority and enthusiasm – a collection of history, investigation, comment, recipes' – Jane Grigson. 'Quite outstanding ... erudite without losing the common touch – or the interest of the reader' – *Spectator*

Josceline Dimbleby's Book of Puddings, Desserts and Savouries

'Full of the most delicious and novel ideas for every type of pudding' – *The Lady*

The Cookery of England   Elisabeth Ayrton

Her fascinating and beautifully compiled history and recipe book of English cooking from the fifteenth century to the present day is 'a lovely book, which could restore pride to our English kitchens' – *The Times Literary Supplement*

FOR THE BEST IN PAPERBACKS, LOOK FOR THE 🐧

FROM THE PENGUIN COOKERY LIBRARY

North Atlantic Seafood   Alan Davidson

'A classic work of reference and a cook's delight' (*The Times Educational Supplement*) from the world's greatest expert on fish cookery. 'Mr Davidson has a gift for conveying memorable information in a way so effortless that his book makes lively reading for its own sake' – Elizabeth David

The Foods and Wines of Spain   Penelope Casas

'I have not come across a book before that captures so well the unlikely medieval mix of Eastern and Northern, earthy and fine, rare and deeply familiar ingredients that make up the Spanish kitchen' – *Harpers and Queen*. 'The definitive book on Spanish cooking … a jewel in the crown of culinary literature' – Craig Claiborne

An Omelette and a Glass of Wine   Elizabeth David

'She has the intelligence, subtlety, sensuality, courage and creative force of the true artist' – *Wine and Food*. 'Her pieces are so entertaining, so original, often witty, critical yet lavish with their praise, that they succeed in enthusing even the most jaded palate' – Arabella Boxer in *Vogue*

English Food   Jane Grigson

'Jane Grigson is perhaps the most serious and discriminating of her generation of cookery writers, and *English Food* is an anthology all who follow her recipes will want to buy for themselves as well as for friends who may wish to know about *real* English food … enticing from page to page' – Pamela Vandyke Price in the *Spectator*

Classic Cheese Cookery   Peter Graham

Delicious, mouth-watering soups, starters, main meals and desserts using cheeses from throughout Europe make this tempting cookery book a must for everyone with an interest in the subject. Clear, informative and comprehensive, it is a book to return to again and again.

BY THE SAME AUTHOR

The F-Plan

Shed pounds with the ease you've dreamed of and feel fitter than ever before as *you* discover why *The F-Plan* changed the eating attitudes of the nation. Britain's top diet-expert, Audrey Eyton reveals how easy it can be to boost your fibre intake, lower your fat intake and eat your way into a slim, fit future. And on meals which can be as simple as beans on toast! Here are the menus, the remarkable health revelations, everything you need to know.

'The most sensational diet of the century' – *Daily Express*

F-Plus

Here are 165 daily F-Plan menus worked out for you, providing your short cut to success on the world's most famous diet. Catering for every lifestyle, Audrey Eyton includes special F-Plan menus for:

- women who lunch at work
- snack-eaters
- keen cooks
- freezer-owners
- busy dieters using convenience foods
- overweight children
- men: drinkers and non-drinkers!

No meal-planning or fibre- and calorie counting is necessary. Here's the even easier way to follow today's faster, healthier, most highly acclaimed diet.

Originally published in hardback under the title, *Even Easier F-Plan*.

BY THE SAME AUTHOR

The F-Plan Calorie and Fibre Chart

Gives you those vital assessments of both calorie and fibre content of everyday foods – so that you can gain the full fibre bonus of easier, speedier weight loss and fitness.

High-fibre canned and packaged foods are listed, together with a separate chart for drinks. Plus a wonderful new selection of effortless five-minute *F-Plan* meals. With the *F-Plan* diet and the *F-Plan Calorie and Fibre Chart* you have an unbeatable recipe for slimming success.

A must for everyone concerned with weight control and health.

also published:

in one volume:

The Complete F-Plan Diet